MURDER IN MAHIM

JERRY PINTO

SPEAKING
TIGER

SPEAKING TIGER PUBLISHING PVT. LTD
4381/4 Ansari Road, Daryaganj,
New Delhi–110002, India

First published in hardback by Speaking Tiger 2017

This revised paperback edition published by Speaking Tiger 2018

ISBN: 978-93-88326-09-4
eISBN: 978-81-933073-7-3

10 9 8 7 6 5 4 3

Typeset in Sabon Roman by SÜRYA, New Delhi
Printed at Sanat Printers, Haryana

Jerry Pinto is a poet, novelist, translator and journalist based in Mumbai. His books include *Em and the Big Hoom* (winner of the Hindu Literary Prize and the Crossword Book Award) and *Helen: The Life and Times of an H-Bomb* (winner of the National Award for the Best Book on Cinema). Among his other works are widely acclaimed translations from Marathi: Daya Pawar's autobiography (*Baluta*); Baburao Bagul's first and classic collection of stories (*When I Hid My Caste*); novels by Sachin Kundalkar (*Cobalt Blue*) and Ganesh Matkari (*Half-open Windows*); and the memoirs of Malika Amar Shaikh (*I Want to Destroy Myself*), Vandana Mishra (*I, the Salt Doll*) and Eknath Awad (*Strike a Blow to Change the World*).

Jerry Pinto was awarded Yale University's Windham-Campbell Prize and the Sahitya Akademi Award in 2016.

Praise for *Murder in Mahim*

'[A] riveting tale...Welcome to the metropolis that the novelist knows like the back of his hand. It's where Peter follows his old friend, Inspector Jende, to find the underbelly of love [and] desire, where men seek out other men...it's a treat to be taken by the hand through the labyrinth of a gripping murder mystery while exploring relationships within families and amongst friends.'—Ganesh Saili, *The New Indian Express*

'[*Murder in Mahim*] takes readers to the gay *addas* of Mumbai with an incisiveness that, as Pinto writes, "would make each individual hair stand upon your head"...[T]he Mumbai of the book is that of Jeet Thayil's *Narcopolis* and Ashok Banker's *Vertigo*, two classics between which this one slides in neatly on the shelf...This is possibly as close to literary fiction as the Subcontinental detective novel has got in the last few years.'—Zac O'Yeah, *Open*

'[A] tightly written crime novel...Pinto has a superb ear for variation, and social anxiety, and the ways in which people shuffle between what they are thinking and what they want to say.'—Arul Mani, *India Today*

'Pinto describes the city with the understatement of a poet. We *feel* the grime of the railway platforms, the impatient traffic, the different kinds of neighbourhoods and homes...[This is] a book one can finish quickly—and then go back to savour again at leisure, a quality few crime novels have[.]'—Peter Griffin, *The Hindu*

'[Pinto's] murder mystery thrills while engaging with perceptions of queer sexuality in India, questions of class and caste, and the lives of sex workers...You can read [*Murder in Mahim*] as a noir mystery that could only be set in Mumbai... Or you could read it as a heart-breaking, searching study about the people that are sucked in and spat out by the city's dark fissures. At its best, the novel can be read and enjoyed as a potent, deft mixture of both.'—Shreya Ila Anasuya, thewire.in

'Reading *Murder in Mahim*, I was reminded of the observation made by Douglas Adams's Dirk Gently that to fully solve a crime, one would need to "solve" the milieu in which it occurred. This book is about the many ways in which a society's underbelly interacts with its mainstream, and the oppression, exploitation—and finally, criminality—that can result. [It] is about the fluidity of gender roles and sex...the thin line between being in control of your sexuality and becoming someone else's puppet; the many unusual and poignant forms that love can take in a time of suppression.'—Jai Arjun Singh, Scroll.in

'[A] page-turner...the author draws you into a world of ageing queens, male prostitutes, corrupt cops and other very well portrayed characters...*Murder in Mahim* succeeds not just because it is a well-plotted whodunit but also because it is a non-judgmental tale of characters rarely cast in Mumbai's hoary narratives.'—Simha Sagar, *Hindustan Times*

MURDER IN MAHIM

Prologue

Bombay doesn't do night. The sun falls into the sea but darkness stands no chance. Every attempt it makes to swallow up the city is defeated by a million neon eyes that open and blink as evening comes; and by the glare of natural gas burning beyond the eastern harbour, illuminating the hill the children call 'Giant's Grave'. Each evening, darkness struggles for footholds and hidey holes.

One of its refuges is the toilet under the bridge at Matunga Road Station on the Western Railway line. The authorities try their best to illuminate it but a small stone is enough to take out the bulb, and by the time an explanation has been made and the requisition has been sanctioned and Stores has disbursed a new bulb, darkness has stayed a while. And for a while it shelters the men who come here, groping each other in the dark, hoping to find some release, perhaps love, or just the warmth of another body.

Darkness will shelter the hunter tonight. Though the crowds on the platforms have thinned, it shouldn't have been so easy to spot his prey. It is a sign. Now he must act quickly.

His prey may not go down to the toilet just yet. He may pretend to be at the station to catch a train and look around for some time. He may even take the train out to Dadar and come back later. But in case he does decide to try his luck right away, it would be good to make sure the place is clear. Even at this hour, there will be men inside. But the hunter knows they are easy to spook. All he has to do is go down to one of the two mouths of the toilet and shout, '*Oey, kya kar rahe ho*!' in as loud, as contemptuous a voice as possible. In that dark, tense silence, no one wants to be asked what he is doing. The toilet empties immediately.

The hunter slips down the slope to the tracks, shouts his magic words, clears the toilet. Then he goes back up again, and positions himself where his prey will see him. Their eyes meet and a flicker of interest lights the other man's face.

The hunter looks around to see if anyone else is watching them. Some of the older men are looking at him hungrily. He opens his eyes wide and raises his eyebrows. They look away hurriedly.

He turns and looks at the young man again. Eye contact is definite, deliberate, clear.

Seconds later, the man is walking down the slope. The hunter follows him, and suddenly, even before he steps into the dark, foetid womb of the toilet, he knows that the moment has come.

One

There was a koel in their bedroom, a persistent and tinny koel. Peter fought his way through layers of sleep, only to realize, somewhere very close to waking, that it was a tone Millie had chosen for her mobile.

He struggled to go back to sleep but now, at fifty-three, his bladder made his early-morning decisions. As Millie groped for the phone, he rolled out of bed and stumbled into the bathroom, the fog of sleep slowly drifting away. He was wide awake when he came back.

'You had better tell your son something,' Millie said.

'What's he done now?' he said, as he took off his home shorts and pulled on a pair of track pants.

'Didn't come home last night. And now he's saying he'll be gone for some time.' She waved her mobile phone at him before replacing it on the bedside table.

'He called?'

'SMS,' she mumbled, curling up again.

Ah yes, the koel was for incoming messages. A quacking duck was her ringtone. It had been funny the first few times; then irritating; now it was just another sound.

'At least he told you this time,' Peter said, playing the devil's advocate. Sunil had a history of disappearing on mysterious errands and trips, almost all of them related to the causes he or his friends at the Tata Institute of Social Sciences espoused. These ranged from relief camps for those afflicted by some natural calamity to a butterfly census in the Sahyadris.

Millie raised her head off the pillow and focussed on him.

'What does "some time" mean? Does it mean some hours? Some days? A week? Teach him communication, why don't you?'

He tried to put on the air of a severe paterfamilias and said: 'I'll have a talk with him when he gets back.'

Millie harrumphed. She had seen that expression before and had come to mistrust it. But she let it go, and Peter slipped out into the morning.

~

The near-dawn air caught his spirits and lifted them. Anyone who had walked into a morning in his city would know that it was the best time of day. The city was about as vulnerable as it could get; it would agree to a compromise, even with the unarmed. And it was cool with the breath of the sea running across it.

Although he paid good money for membership in a gym, Peter preferred to walk at Shivaji Park when he could. He liked the open air and the red mud, the incidental beauty of sonchafa crushed underfoot. The centre of the park was bare at this time, empty but for a few dogs and some elderly men trying to keep their joints flexible. Later, it would crowd up with a hundred cricket matches and in the winter, even a scratch diamond would be set up and NRI kids would steal second base as bemused spectators watched silently. Shivaji Park, the heartland of conservative Maharashtriana, was changing.

Two tribal boys were filling plastic mineral water bottles with honey from a hive high up in a tree on the south side. They offered to sell him a full bottle for only a hundred rupees; Peter was tempted but had no cash with him. He walked on, past the Nana-Nani Park where once the morning laughter club had met. No one was there. Had they been driven away by the local owls?

On Cadell Road, the traffic hooted and roared but it was not yet a river of metal. Past the mayor's bungalow, a one-eyed dog yawned politely at him. Peter yawned back.

On the second round, his knees told him it was time to head back. His gut sought surcease and his stomach was asking for a banana. He made for home.

And he knew as he walked into the house that the tenor of the day had changed.

Millie was at the dining table. She looked up from the newspaper she was reading, and her face was filled with a terrible rage.

'So this is why you sent him to do social work?'

Out of habit, Peter felt he should apologize. For some reason, Sunil's misdeeds had always been put down to his account, and now, as always, he argued his case in his head: 'I didn't send him anywhere, he went of his own accord.' But there was too much emotion in Millie's tone to allow him to interpose with a rational remark. Now she tossed the evening paper—which always came *before* the morning papers—on the table in front of him. He picked it up. There was his son, arm in arm with a hijra on one side and an obese man on the other. The obese man's T-shirt said 'Gay and proud of it'. Sunil was wearing a rainbow-striped bandanna. The hijra was in a sari that revealed hints of blue under clouds of silver zari.

'This means nothing...' Peter began.

'Read underneath!' Millie cut in.

Peter read:

Gay activist Sunil Fernandes leads protests at Maheshwari Udyan against the Supreme Court's verdict yesterday which reversed the Delhi High Court's judgement reading down Section 377 of the Indian Penal Code...

'I don't know...' he began again and found that he could not end the sentence.

But now his gut would not wait any longer and he took the paper with him into the loo, forsaking his usual staple toilet reading: a book of poetry.

Gay activist Sunil Fernandes.

'Gay' was an adjective, of course. It could describe the activism that his son was involved in. Or it could describe his...

No, his mind said. Not Sunil.

He looked for a report but there was nothing. These days a picture could pass for a story. He knew that the Delhi High Court's verdict in 2009 on reading down Section 377 that criminalized homosexuality, even between consenting adults, had been greeted with delight. Four years later, the Supreme Court had played kill-joy and once again, India had returned to the company of countries like North Korea, Iraq and Syria where homosexuality was still illegal. Protests had broken out in many parts of the country.

Obviously Sunil had gone along to show solidarity. It was the kind of thing he would do. It was the kind of thing he *should* do, surely?

Peter was still mulling this when he returned to the dining table and applied himself mechanically to his bowl of banana and *dahi*. Millie was sitting as he had left her. He looked up and caught her glance. She was waiting for him to say something. She was hoping he would clear it all up, willing him to make it go away.

Dutifully, he tried.

'There must be some mistake,' he said. 'When he went to protest the death penalty, it was not because he was a murderer.'

Millie took the paper from him and looked at it again. Then she shook her head.

'This is not the way,' she said and went into the kitchen.

Not the way? Did she mean this was not the way Sunil should have let them know about his sexuality? Again, something in Peter's mind said: No, not Sunil.

He challenged it: Why not Sunil?

But it stubbornly repeated the same phrase. He silenced it and looked down at the tabloid.

Gay activist Sunil Fernandes...

What did it mean, really? The easy thing would be to call Sunil and find out.

He dialled his son's number.

A professionally cheerful woman's voice said that the number was out of reach. As she began to repeat the message in another language, he disconnected and set himself a task.

Confront it, he said. Think about it.

Gay.

He tried saying it to himself in his head. 'Sunil is gay.' It didn't seem to make sense, it didn't connect with him. It was as if he were inside a bubble, his eyes sealed and ears plugged.

He tried again. 'My son is gay.' But again there was no emotional response. He could as well have said: 'The sky is blue.' And yet the day had changed completely. The picture, the bandanna, his son's gaze, the caption produced a hollowness in his shoulders, above his lungs. So it is not the day that has changed, he told himself, it is you who have changed.

He called Sunil's number again and got the same response.

Millie came out of the kitchen, her face reconstructed in tight lines, evidence of her determination not to show any emotion. Peter couldn't bear it. He went up to her and hugged her. She resisted a little as she always did and then relaxed into him, again as she always did. Then she was overcome and began to cry, her body heaving. Peter wanted to cry too. They stood like that and he wondered what else he could say, what else he could do.

My son is gay. My wife is sad about it. I am sad too. Am I sad because my wife is sad? Or am I sad because I don't want to have a gay son?

Peter had never thought of himself as homophobic. He had worked with gay men and he had seen that some were hard-drinking and foul-mouthed reporters; others were camp and fay and talked about going to the little girls' room when they wanted to pee. They were people and they came in all stripes and colours and political persuasions. He had liked some and disliked some and he had thought that this meant he was not homophobic even if he himself was not interested.

'Okay?' he asked when Millie reached into her housecoat pocket for a hankie to honk into. 'Let's have a cuppa and try to think.'

Millie sighed.

'You make tea if you want.'

'You don't want?'

'No, what's the use?' she asked rhetorically. 'His whole life...' she began but couldn't bring herself to finish and started afresh: 'I only thought...' But she could not complete this either. 'What did we...' There seemed to be no words. Or at least none that felt right.

'I think I'll have that tea.' He got up.

'No, you make soup and say it's tea. I'll make it. You sit. What else is new?'

At least these were familiar complaints. He followed her into the kitchen and sat at the table.

'See, Millie...'

She rounded on him. 'Don't take that tone with me.'

'What tone?'

'Condescending. As if I'm a child and you're a teacher.'

'Okay. I don't think he's...like that.'

'See? You can't even say it.'

'Okay. I don't think he's homosexual. I think he's supporting a cause.'

'This is the only cause he could find?'

'Well, it could be worse.'

'How?'

Peter fell silent. Already, he had suggested that being gay was bad. He was not going to dig himself in any further. Millie poured warm water into the pot and swilled it about before tossing it out. She measured out tea leaves with the air of an alchemist. She did not usually turn tea-drinking into a ceremony Okakura Kakuzo would have approved of but Peter could see that she needed something to distract her mind.

They sat at the table, sipping, when Millie suddenly said: 'I want to be a grandmother.'

Peter wanted to say, 'And so you shall be,' because he loved her—and the thought surprised him. He wanted to reassure her but he could not.

'You know, Peter,' Millie said, 'you could sometimes, just sometimes, say something comforting even if it isn't true.'

'I don't know how to do that,' he said.

'Easy,' she said. 'Just lie.'

He smiled and they sipped some more. He tasted the fineness of Yunnan but only at a distance, with no pleasure.

'Talk to him,' she said. 'He's your son.'

He wanted to say, 'Why me? Why not you? Isn't he your son too?' but he didn't. Masculinity had certain prerogatives. One of these was that if there was a crisis of whatever kind, you had to step up or you had to find someone to step up. It was time to step up. He dialled Sunil. The chirpy voice began to make its regretful speech.

'Switched off,' he said.

'As though that's a surprise,' she said and brooded a while, sipping her tea. Then she asked, 'What will you say?'

'I don't know.'

'Then why talk?'

Peter shrugged and Millie sighed.

The phone rang. It was Jende.

'Come,' he said.

~

It sounded like a summons but it was not. Peter had taken early voluntary retirement from a newspaper that wanted no unionized employees on its rolls. With only a mild feeling of guilt, he had accepted the handsome retrenchment package that allowed him now to live on the interest with careful inroads into the capital. A few months after he left, a murder had taken place at the gym where he worked out in a somewhat unconvinced fashion after a cholesterol scare, and he had reconnected with an old school friend, Shiva, now Inspector Jende of the Mahim Police Station. This was a world very different from the ones in which he had lived but he was fascinated by the oddness of it, by the moment that turned a law-abiding citizen into a criminal. Perhaps because of the ease with which he could chat to perfect strangers, or because he was better company than policemen, Jende sometimes included him in the less routine investigations.

By the tone of Jende's voice now, he knew it was murder.

'Where?' he asked, glad to get a chance to get out of the house.

'Matunga Road Station bridge.'

Peter rose from the table. 'Okay. Coming.'

'Where you're going now?' Millie asked.

'Shiva called.'

'Ah. So you must go.'

Millie was not sure she liked his association with Jende but she knew that a man had to have an interest and he had to get out of the house. Besides, it was always useful to be friends with a cop.

'I can tell him...'

'No, no,' said Millie. 'Go.'

She sighed but it was not an angry sigh. It was the sigh of the young woman he had fallen in love with, the sigh of the young woman who had majored in philosophy, studied it angrily because so many of the thinkers she loved could not find a place for the God she loved just as passionately. He had asked her how she could be reading Nietzsche just before going to Mass, and she had said, 'Render unto the University the things that are the University's and render unto God the things that are God's.'

He had laughed, for it was easy to laugh then and it charmed him to be laughing at something a beautiful girl in a summer dress said, as they sat on the lawns of the university, eating grapes she had brought from Nashik after paying a visit to the Shrine of the Infant Jesus.

Perhaps she needed some time to think. Or to cry again. He needed time too, and Jende would have something to distract him.

Two

Peter walked slowly down Takandas H. Kataria Marg that led to the Matunga Road Station. It was a street he had walked every day for years on his way to the newspaper, and he often came back for a stroll post 'retirement' because he missed the aromas. The smell of jaggery and spiced cashews from the Mangalore shop. The gummy reek of a jackfruit cut open by the Bihari vendor. The heady scents of incense and ghee and marigolds from the Saptakoteshwara Temple. The sharp tang of Gauri, the black cow tethered outside the temple.

He stopped to stroke Gauri, and she shifted a little to stand closer to him. He wanted to linger, to savour her friendliness. But he had to go; Shiva would be waiting.

Why had Shiva called him? Why was he going? Most people did not want to get involved with criminal affairs. He could understand why. Go too close and you might find yourself in a witness box or something worse. Should he have simply told Shiva that he was busy? What would have happened then? 'You can walk away whenever you want,' he said to himself bracingly. 'This is not your job. Or your life work.'

Perhaps that was why he did go when Shiva called. Because it was possible for him to say no.

A horn beeped. Even in the morning with a clear road, the drivers of the city felt the need to honk. But he realized that he was at the intersection of Gopi Tank Road and Kataria

Marg. As a child, he had spent hours here, hanging over the edge of the well at the Manmala Devi Mandir, peering into its cool black depths, watching a turtle or two dip and glide among the leaves of banyan and mango that had fallen from above. There must have been a level crossing where the road met the railway tracks but Peter could not remember it now. At some point, a pedestrian bridge had been built over the tracks.

Even from the top of the pedestrian bridge, jammed with hawkers and busy feet, Peter saw where he would have to go. There was a knot of people on the tracks, spilling out from under the bridge where Peter could see signs of police presence. He thought about buying a platform ticket but decided against it; he was on police business. He found Inspector Jende standing at the foot of the ramp that came down off the bridge on to the two platforms of the station.

'Pittr,' said Jende. It was his greeting of choice.

'Ah,' said Peter. 'There you are.'

There was a railway official in a battered black coat talking fast, in the hurried way men have when they are out of their depth.

'On this platform, we have one toilet at the south end with ladies facility and one gents facility for squatting. One gents facility here at this end, but only gents urinal,' he was saying, in a mix of Marathi and English.

Jende absorbed this information. Then: 'Is that one also open all night?'

'Yes. Means no, means yes.'

Jende raised an eyebrow.

'Means it has a gate and a lock and key so it can be locked but often it is not and I think last night it was not locked.'

'No *laash* there, na?'

So there was a corpse somewhere. Presumably in the toilet under the stone bridge at the end of the station. Peter had used it a couple of times, reluctantly, when he couldn't wait till he got home. This 'gents facility' had no gate; the stalls were ranged against one wall of a passage cut through the slope of the ramp from the bridge.

Meanwhile, the railway official had gone from shell-shocked to aghast at the thought of another corpse in his station.

'I have not checked.'

'Better check.'

The railway official looked carefully at Jende to see if this was a joke. Then he decided not to risk it and hurried off. Peter looked reprovingly at Jende. Jende shrugged.

'Look at this situation,' said Jende, waving a hand at the city and switching to his preferred language, a no-nonsense, Marathi-inflected Hindi. He didn't seem angry, just vaguely irritated. 'The station is open all night. There is no gate anywhere. Any person can come and go. If you want to climb over that wall'—he pointed east to where low-slung government quarters, painted white and blue, slumped under the weight of clothes drying in the small balconies—'or over that tree'—he pointed west to where Tulsi Pipe Road ran parallel to the railway lines, 'you can come and go and do *khoon-kharaaba* of all kinds, and who will look?'

'Khoon-kharaaba?'

'One khoon, at least. Come. You had breakfast?'

'Some.'

'Good. After this you may not feel like any.'

Together they walked down the short slope that dropped from the platform to the tracks. The sharp smell of urine assailed Peter's nostrils, that and the smell of the railways. What was it? The tang of iron. It had been on his hands after every strap-hanging commute. But it was also the smell of blood, spilled and decaying. Haemoglobin decomposing, rusting. Blood rusts, he thought, just as the railways do.

They passed what looked like a room built into the bridge, a cave-like room with no windows and which had not been used for decades, it seemed, from the dirt and debris inside. Then came the toilet and inside it, a young man lay on his back, his body sprawled on the half-wet floor.

'See?' Jende said. 'You can come in this side and go out that side. No doors, no gates, nothing. Everything open-air.'

Peter saw what he meant: Matunga Road Station was a policing nightmare. Right now, the dead boy constituted the nightmare. But in his moment at the centre of things, he looked relaxed, one leg crossed over the other, one arm thrown up over his head. He was slim and dressed in knock-off fashion, his hair in an undercut. An earring glinted in one ear. It was easy to see what had killed him. A slash had opened his shirt (a dark colour), his banian (once white but now almost black with clotted blood), his skin (brown), the fatty layer underneath (a bright shade of yellow), his innards (purple and red, what might once have been described as incarnadine). The body had been outlined in chalk. A photographer was walking away, his face pasty.

'What a terrible place to die,' Peter said.

'Dead is dead,' said Jende.

Two *jamadars*—what was the term for them now, Peter thought? Class IV staff? Or did the morgue still use the old designations?—came up with a stretcher. The men loaded the body without a word or a sign of emotion. He might have been a slab of dead meat. The dead man's arm fell off the stretcher. Peter moved forward without thinking and pushed it back onto the body. The skin was cold and wet and clammy. It did not feel human.

'Don't touch,' Jende said.

'Oh yes, I shouldn't contaminate the scene.'

'For him? Who will care?'

Peter looked at his friend carefully.

'Then why am I here?'

'Same reason I am here. Because he died before his time and I will find out who did this to him.'

Peter looked again at the young face. It suggested relief, in an odd way. Could it only be the way muscles lost their tension in death? Or was it just that his eyes were half-closed, the irises dark smudges against slits of white?

The body was about to be whisked away when the constables holding the public back moved aside, in the manner of those acknowledging their supervisors. Two men appeared and both their faces had, for a moment, looks of shock and horror.

'Pagmat? Durra?'

Now, confronted by Jende, both men had almost identical sheepish expressions. Peter guessed that they were also policemen, but off duty. Their polyester shirts were unlined, their foreheads creased with the professional scowl of the city policeman. Almost certainly not constables, but not Inspectors either. They looked to be in their mid thirties—the older of the two perhaps closer to forty. Sub-Inspectors, then? And if they were policemen, were they not hardened by death? Why had they looked horrified? Or could it be that he was expecting uniformed men to be...Peter scolded himself silently for stereotyping.

One of them said, 'Body?'

Jende nodded. Then he looked from one to the other: 'What are you doing here?'

'Like that only,' said the younger of the two, but it was weak. He was finding it difficult to believe his own excuse. His eyes kept shifting towards the body and back, as if he were doing something he was not allowed to.

Peter had an odd feeling and then Jende voiced it when he asked: 'Some relation of yours, Pagmat?'

Pagmat blinked.

'*Kya sahib*!' he said. 'He was a *chhakka*.'

The older cop's head whipped around. Pagmat looked at him out of the side of his eye and blinked again.

'Durra?' Jende asked but Durra only shook his head.

Chhakka, the catch-all word to mean that the dead man wasn't a heterosexual as they understood heterosexuality. But how did they know he was gay or bisexual or whatever? To Peter he looked like a million other young men he walked among in the city every day. But for the brutal gash that had killed him.

It was the question Jende was also asking.

'How do you know?'

Pagmat put on the face of a man unjustly accused.

'Matunga Road, sahib. Famous.'

'Famous for what?' Peter asked.

The men looked puzzled, as if unsure about how they should answer him. Then Pagmat said, 'They come to do *gandugiri*.'

Another word for homosexuality. If chhakka was ridicule, this was contempt.

'Look at his clothes,' said Durra.

Both Jende and Peter turned to look, as directed, at the clothes of the fallen. The young man was wearing a tight black T-shirt with the sleeves rolled up high on his arms and form-fitting, low-rise jeans. Peter thought: half the boys in the city dress like that.

Jende nodded at the men, but maintained his air of being unsatisfied with their explanations.

'Take him away,' he said to the men with the stretcher.

'Did you find his mobile?' Durra asked. Peter happened to be looking at Pagmat's face and saw a moment of murderous rage cross it. Some line had been crossed, some agreement broken.

Jende halted the procession and pulled on a glove and drew from the boy's pocket a blood-drenched instrument.

'Wow,' said Peter, to whom the phone looked rather expensive.

Jende was dismissive. 'China stuff,' he said. Then noticing the two men's eyes on him, he raised his eyebrows. Durra flicked Pagmat an apologetic look as they turned to leave.

Jende waited, watching them, his face impassive. Then he beckoned Peter and climbed on to the platform again. He rinsed the phone off under a tap at the water fountain. A passing commuter shuddered and asked, '*Mara kya?*' but like Jesting Pilate, he did not wait for an answer. Another one asked if the man had been cut fully into two. A man in a white Gandhi cap came up and simply watched the blood run off, silent, thoughtful, almost meditative. Jende ignored all of them and tried to power up the phone. It refused to light up.

'Put it in a bucket of rice,' said the meditative man. A train thundered in and he ran off.

Jende gave up. '*Chalo*, we will need experts,' he said.

Jende hated experts. Of all the experts, he hated experts in electronics and the world of telephony the most. And yet they had led to more arrests than ever before. It seemed as if everyone left a trail across cyberspace, however careful they were in the real world.

'Do we know who the dead man is?'

'No,' said Jende.

'Wallet?'

'Not carrying.'

'Maybe the phone will tell us.'

'If it is his phone. It might be stolen.'

There was a pause as Peter considered this.

'There is CCTV on MRU,' said Jende.

'Really? Since when?'

'They installed them after the blasts.'

Peter flashed back to that day in July 2006 when a series of bombs exploded on the commuter trains in a coordinated terror attack. In the newsroom, they had debated whether to do a spirit-of-Mumbai story for the next morning. Eventually the story had been carried, although it was written in a deliberately colourless manner, the reporter's protest against a story that he did not want to do. But if any good could be said to have come of that terrible day, some money had been sanctioned by the Centre to upgrade the trains. The closed-circuit television cameras must have been part of that.

'For that too we'll need experts. I will go and deal with experts. But first come, look at this.'

They walked back down into the toilet and Jende pointed to the wall above the spot where the body had lain. Peter saw the numeral '1', written in some dark colour. He went up as close as he dared but couldn't be sure.

'Is it blood?' he asked.

'We'll find out,' said Jende. 'They've taken a sample.'

'The man who did this is planning more?'

Jende nodded. 'At least that is what he wants someone to know. Who is this message for, that is what I want to know.'

They walked out of the toilet. 'I will go and write my report now,' said Jende.

It was a dismissal. Peter turned his steps home and as he did, the boy faded and his own family came surging back. In vain did he try to fix his mind on the murder. A man's life had been taken and he was bothered about his son appearing in a tabloid with a caption underneath that declared him gay.

On his way home, he looked at the men he passed. Was anyone of them gay? He remembered India's first gay rights crusader, Ashok Row Kavi, claiming that ten per cent of India was gay. That was a lot of gay people. On what basis had he made that estimate? And how little it seemed to matter now—whether one of a hundred million or a hundred thousand, his son would…'What?' he asked himself aloud, and an elderly woman walking in the opposite direction stopped to look at him in some alarm. Embarrassed, he walked on. 'Sunil will what?' he asked himself silently again, and as he answered his own question, his heart constricted: 'He will suffer.' And then he dismissed the thought. *No. Sunil is not alone. He has Millie, he has me.*

At home Millie was in an even worse mood if this were possible.

'What happened?' he asked.

'He's gone now.'

'Who?'

'Who? You're asking *who*?'

For a moment Peter was afraid she might explode.

'Sunil?'

'Yes,' Millie said and waved her old Nokia phone at him. He read Sunil's message: 'Gone 4 a few days 2 NE. Urgnt n prsnl. Will try 2 call but prolly b out of range. Dnt worry. That's an order. S'

'Okay,' he said.

'Is that all you have to say?' Millie demanded.

Something snapped inside him. 'What do you want me to do? Go and drag him back? He's an adult, Millie. And we have to get used to that.'

'Why are you shouting?' Millie asked but her voice was much more reasonable now.

He wanted to say, 'Because you were,' but he knew from long experience that no one ever knows they are shouting. He hadn't known. Instead, he managed a sorry but it came out strangled. Millie sniffed.

'Cup of tea?' she asked, well-versed in the keeping of harmony in a small flat where the walls could be relied upon to carry all sounds of discord into the neighbouring homes.

'Lovely,' he said.

He went into the kitchen with her, his own small gesture of amity.

'What if he is gay?' he asked of her back. It seemed easier to ask this of her back.

'Oh don't use that word. It was such a nice word.'

He accepted this as a placeholder while she thought out her answer.

'Homosexual, then. What if Sunil is homosexual?'

'Was it for this the clay grew tall?' she asked. He recognized the line from Wilfred Owen. He remembered his mother reading the poem and weeping at the funeral when her brother came home in a coffin from the 1971 war.

'No,' Millie said suddenly, her voice violent with self-reproach. 'I shouldn't talk like that. Is sex the only thing in the world?'

She was now talking to herself, persuading herself. Peter thought he should add something too. 'He's a good boy. He fights for the rights of the...'

'There are no other things to fight for?'

'We all choose our battles,' he said.

She shrugged a little. 'Yes, and I suppose he chose one that was close to him.'

She thumped a tin down in front of him.

'Put.'

He opened it and found chunks of jaggery inside. No sugar. Another of Sunil's recommendations. Sugar was cancer food, he said. Everything is cancer food these days, Millie had replied huffily, but had switched to jaggery powder. Too many chemicals used to make it powder and keep it powder, Sunil had said. Who died and left you his MBBS? his mother had demanded but had changed to jaggery chunks, and an ice pick to break pieces off them.

They took their cups into the hall and settled down into armchairs, their spines folding into bamboo and cloth-stuffing. A peanut floated to the top of Peter's tea. Peanuts got into everything in Maharashtra. He tilted the cup to show it to Millie and won a reluctant smile from her. He took a large sip and the peanut vanished. They sipped and thought, sipped and tried not to think. It was impossible to think; it was impossible not to.

'I suppose one can live without grandchildren also,' Millie said suddenly. She was looking at him.

'Peter?'

'Yes,' he said.

'Don't you want grandchildren?'

He began to pick his way through the minefield.

'Of course, like everyone else...'

'You don't want grandchildren,' she cut in, incredulous. He wanted to tell her she was wrong but he knew that he would be lying. Long ago, he had decided that he would not lie to her unless there was a very good reason. He could think of none now.

'Why not?' There was disappointment in her surprise.

'I haven't thought about it.'

'Haven't thought?' she all but snorted. 'You?'

This could even be construed as a compliment but not in that tone of voice.

'Is it about growing old?'

He did not think it was. From the look she gave him, it was clear she didn't think so either. She waited. And as he tried to conjure up some response, he found himself thinking of the dead boy. He too must have been a baby once. A line from a Keki Daruwalla poem floated into his head.

Always when the foal is born
night is over
  it is dawn.

A baby is like a flood of hope, and then comes a night and a blade and the moon is blood. He wondered how to tell Millie this. She had shared his love of poetry but for some strange reason, they had stopped reading it together. One more casualty of marriage. One more casualty of being a parent. And yet Sunil had brought so much with him, so much joy. He could still remember the first time he had held Sunil and wondered at how everything inside him seemed the same and yet how it was all shifting and sliding and changing, something immense happening, a tectonic shift in his identity that was linking him to this tiny screaming scrap of humanity, its red face already a reproach to his skills as a parent.

He did not know how he could tell Millie that he was not sure he could take such a risk again, if he could expose himself to such vulnerability. Each day the newspaper brought fresh horror stories: the child abused on the bus, the child who fell down a manhole, the child who died in the toilet imprisoned by some power-maddened teacher. Everything that could go wrong seemed to go wrong and it always happened to children. Face-down in the mass grave, shell-shocked by the bomb, child after child.

'Oh never mind,' said Millie. 'Why bother with what we cannot have.'

Then she began to cry. Peter gave her a clumsy hug and held her for a while.

'Chhah,' she said. 'This is stupid.'

'That's the spirit,' he said.

'At least you didn't call me Old Girl,' she said and took a big swig of tea. It was an old joke between them. Early in their courtship, she had told him about Miss Bertha, an Anglo-Indian teacher at her school who had been in the habit of consoling losers with 'Buck up, old fruit' and 'That's the spirit, old girl'. Those phrases had entered a lexicon of intimacy easily; he had used them at first ironically to show her he cared, to show her he remembered things she told him, even the useless odd things and their sources.

'And if anyone asks, I'll say, what business is it of yours?' she said now.

Peter saw that this was another angle. Other people. How did one face the neighbours? How did one face the parish? How did one face one's friends? Not that it was any of their concern, technically speaking, but this was not a technicality. This was about what your son did in bed and how it was now public information. And Millie was much more connected to all these worlds than he was and so she would suffer their slights and rejections more deeply.

After lunch, Millie curled up into a ball for a nap but Peter was restless. He decided to go for a walk. His footsteps took him to the police station.

Jende was just getting off the phone, his face grim.

'Something?'

'Kidney. They took that boy's kidney.'

'Organ-trade-walas?'

'Forensics says no. No one will take a kidney in the middle of a toilet. Too much risk of infection.'

'Do these people care?'

Jende shrugged. 'It's about supply and demand. If you start bringing kidneys that have been taken out in toilets, who is going to ask you again?'

That made sense. Peter cast about.

'Maybe they took it somewhere else…'

No, that couldn't be. But Jende was already all over it.

'Yes, they cut him in a nice clean hotel room and took his kidney and they collected up the blood and they came and threw it in the toilet with the body.'

Peter raised a hand to acknowledge his stupidity.

Were they dealing with a serial killer, then? A fetishist? Someone who took trophies? All those grisly *CSI* stories from the television suddenly seemed uncomfortably close to home. But wary of being insulted for his amateur status again, Peter kept his mouth shut. Jende was talking aloud, feeling his way through:

'Besides, forensics says it was not a clean cut.'

'Means?'

Jende leaned back.

'If you're used to cutting, you do it like *that*,' and here he slashed his hand through the air as if using a whip. 'You know what you're doing. You know that something may come in the way. Inside the body, there's this bone, that part, this muscle, that thing...you know this and you know you have to make it quick—take the knife—*zweeen*—all the way through. Or you do this,' here he suggested a quick jab. 'But for this you have to be sure. You must know, inside here, the heart. I'm taking the heart. In-out. Like that. But this is a first-time person. This is the first time he's cutting, possibly the first time he's killing. So he cuts and thinks, "Enough," and then he cuts again and then it's easier because the man is now almost finished, and so he makes it bigger. With his hand.'

'But what was the victim doing?'

'He did not struggle. We don't know why. Like he was willing to let this happen.'

Peter thought of the boy's face, how he had seemed relieved almost.

Jende's frown got deeper. 'So this is a first-time killer who writes in blood on the wall. Yes, it was blood. The boy's blood.'

A first-time killer. Why did that seem reassuring? From all that Peter had read, the first murder was supposed to be the difficult one. After that it got easy. Where had he read that? Surely not Agatha Christie...Would this man strike again? And why are you calling the murderer a man? he asked himself. It could have been a woman. But the answer to that was easy: it was a male toilet.

'I think this kidney taking is important,' he said.

'Like on television? Someone is mental and likes to take things from the body and all?'

'Sort of.'

'Chhah. I don't think it's like that,' said Jende. 'I think it's a moment of insanity, that moment when he has cut and there's blood coming, *chhikk-chikk*, and he thinks "Chalo, I'll pull something out" and he reaches in and pulls and throws.'

What manner of man was this? A first-time killer who could reach into a dead man and pull out a kidney. What drove his hand? What slowed his knife? And how did he know where to find the kidney? Did he cut it out or was it animal like, fingers and nails for teeth? Peter shuddered, and hoped his friend hadn't noticed.

'Has the kidney been found?'

'No.'

'Has there been a search?'

'As if you'll find. It's a piece of meat, Pittr. You know it's a human kidney. The killer knows it's a human kidney. The street dog knows? The crow knows? Does that bird, you know the one who used to take our vada pao in school in the recess, right out of our hands, that bird, he knows?'

Peter waited for this to pass. He'd asked for it.

'The dogs, the cheels, the rats, they don't see it as evidence. You throw something away in this city and it's gone. Maybe he flung it somewhere in the toilet, maybe on the tracks. Maybe he even walked with it all the way to Mahim Creek. He could have walked down the tracks in the night with it in his hand and who would be there to see?'

Peter looked at him.

'Okay, joking. Maybe not Mahim Creek.'

'But there's something not right…' Peter began.

'You think he's mental?'

'If not mental, then somewhat deranged. Something has brought his madness to the surface. Here's a first-time killer with a knife, you say. You'd think he'd be very startled by all that blood, by what he did. Instead, he reaches into the body and takes a kidney?'

'I don't know, Pittr. It's too filmy for me. But you may even be right. *Duniya tedhi hai*, everything is simple and everything is mixed up. We do our best. So try your theory. If you want to meet someone to talk about it, go see Dr Ajit Pitale. I'll give you his card. He's a psychiatrist and advises the courts when there's some question of madness in a case.'

Jende rooted about on his desk and pulled out a card. His body language was clear: you're welcome to waste your time. Peter took the card anyway and stuck it in his pocket.

'What do we know about the victim?' he asked.

'L.S. Parthusta. Age twenty-four. Address: Railway Quarters, Elphinstone Road.'

'Anything else?'

'Nothing that we know. But something we can guess. On the CCTV, he's going in and out of the toilet ten-ten times in one hour.'

'So he must have been...'

'A bender.'

A bender. Peter had not heard that phrase since he and Shiva had been at school and the effeminate among them had been so described. He had never questioned the term then; now he thought it probably had something to do with assuming the position. He suppressed the thought of Sunil being called a bender. And then the sudden terrible thought: *Was this his world? Was this how he...?*

'Probably doing business,' Jende added.

'Business?'

'*Randigiri*. Sex trade we must say now. I'm going to his place. Coming?'

There was nothing better to do.

'Chalo,' Peter said.

Three

The chawl was not like one of the older mill chawls, which sometimes had character with their wide airy verandas and their angular staircases that made them look like Escher prints. This one was of government construction, Public Works Department of the 1960s or thereabouts, and its residents would struggle all their lives to maintain some semblance of dignity as they queued up outside the common toilets each day.

L.S. Parthusta had lived on the third floor. It was easy to identify the family of the bereaved: the women were sitting outside, weeping or in positions that suggested they had been weeping. Jende flashed his identity card though it didn't even seem necessary.

Inside an old man was lying down on a cot that seemed to be built into the wall.

'Who is it?' he asked. 'My son? Has my Lachhman come back to me?'

The lines were out of a Bollywood potboiler. But that, Peter reminded himself, was also what art of any kind taught us to do: to express emotions. He thought of Grahame Greene in hospital, listening to a bereaved parent mourning the loss of a child and thinking that she was spouting nothing but clichés. That the old man's grief was real could not be denied. That he was borrowing his dramaturgy from Bollywood was also true. One did not negate the other.

'Police,' said Jende and looked around helplessly. 'Where are his things?'

The old man pointed upwards. 'Please,' thought Peter, 'no philosophy. Not now.'

But the old man had not been suggesting anything other than a physical direction. The family had added a loft, a *maalya* it was called. A ladder was folded against the wall and when it opened out, it reached the square trapdoor perfectly, slotting elegantly into two notches in front of the trap door.

Jende pulled at the door. It was locked.

The old man said: 'He would lock it when he went out.'

Jende looked at the old man again.

'Did he pay rent?'

The old man was shocked at the suggestion.

'My blood,' he said, raising his head off the cot with an effort. 'He is my blood. Will I take rent from my blood?'

'Your blood locks his door. That's why I'm asking,' said Jende. 'Who was he to you?'

A tear ran down the side of the old man's face, into his scanty sideburns.

'Grandson,' he said.

Jende spoke in a gentler voice.

'Where are the keys?'

No one seemed to know.

'Get me a hammer.'

Someone was sent off to fetch one.

'He was working somewhere?'

'He was trying for a job. But you know how it is. These people have taken over. Bengalis. These days only Bengalis get jobs. We are out.'

Only Bengalis get jobs? Peter wondered. Then the penny dropped: in the railways.

'You have to know people to get in. He was a good boy.'

At this point someone walked in with a hammer and Jende

swung it, breaking lock and latch in one shot. This seemed to be the last straw for the old man who dropped his head back onto the cot and burst into noisy tears. They ascended to the soundtrack of his sobbing.

Peter went up first and was engulfed by a peculiar odour; at once intensely familiar and totally different. Some of it was unwashed clothes—of which there was a considerable pile—and some of it was a cheap perfume. A knock-off version of Brut or Denim, cooked up in a warehouse in Ulhasnagar, guaranteed to decompose within ten minutes of spraying. Jende kicked piles of clothes aside; he meant no disrespect; it was the only way to navigate around the room.

'Odd,' said Peter, looking around. He had placed the smell. It was the smell of a male hostel room in a college.

'What?'

'All these dirty clothes.'

'Boys are like that.'

'Yes. When they're not living at home.'

Jende stopped.

'This is his home. His permanent address on the aadhaar card.'

'Okay. But in my home, in your home, in anyone's home, someone will come and do the washing, right? I mean, it's your mother or wife or...' he realized that this was beginning to sound sexist 'or someone...'

'Your bai,' said Jende who was not much bothered by these finer points.

'Or your houseman,' Peter said, flailing.

'So? Short point?'

'Why are there so many dirty clothes here?'

'He keeps it locked. How will anyone take the clothes to wash?'

'Why didn't he just throw them down?'

'Too lazy?'

'All he had to do was kick them out of the door.'

'For some boys I know, even this will be too much work,' said Jende feelingly. He had two sons.

'No,' Peter said. 'Not young men. They like clean clothes.'

He took a few steps and came up against the roof. There was not much room.

'He locked it up. He must have wanted to keep his family out. There is something here. Something he wanted hidden,' he said.

Jende looked at him for a moment and then said: 'So we must find what he wanted to hide,' and he began by pushing some of the dirty clothes into a corner with his foot. This was a gesture. For everywhere there were dirty clothes: shirts, underwear, banians, trousers, jeans, shorts and Capri-length shorts. Both of them worked at it and soon everything was in one heap in a corner.

'Lots of clothes,' said Peter.

'They are his work clothes,' said Jende.

Peter nodded. The rest of the young man's possessions did not amount to much: a Parker pen set, a file of school and college certificates attesting to mediocre-to-poor performance in academics; another file with three copies of a CV made some years ago and signed with a flourish; some unsigned greeting cards of immense florality and size, a can of deodorant and a jar of mauve hair mousse, some condoms, an iPod and earphones, a mobile phone charger, three years of the *Manorama Yearbook,* a handbook titled 'How to pass the banking examinations', and a quantity of photographs taken at some college picnic. Jende took the photographs.

There was nothing out of the ordinary.

'Okay, where are his bank books?' Jende asked. 'I can't find any *bank ka saamaan.*'

'Money? Where does he keep his money?' Peter asked and looked again at the clothes. The unwashed clothes. Unwashed clothes in a house where the women would happily wash, dry, starch, iron, repair...

He picked up a long-sleeved shirt whose sleeves were rolled up and for an odd moment felt it was all wrong. He looked at it carefully. Ah. Sunil had the same shirt. Is that it? Just that my son and this boy have the same shirt? He thought of the aesthete Richard Lannoy, whom he had interviewed in the 1990s, telling him of a visit to Banaras in the 1950s: 'You could tell where each person came from, down to the village, from what they were wearing. You could even tell the caste. But this time, everyone was in polyester.' The wash-and-wear revolution made it possible for the resident of a chawl and the resident of a flat to wear the same clothes. He was about to put the shirt down when some sense—what was it? In his hands? His arms?—some sense told him that there was something else.

It was heavier than it should be.

He shook the shirt and putting his hands into it, turned it inside out.

Nothing.

He shook it vigorously. Nothing fell out. But the sleeves were still rolled up. He unrolled one and a small bundle of thousand-rupee notes fell out. The other sleeve contained a similar bundle.

'Jende?'

Jende swept all the clothes into one corner of the room and both he and Peter began to strip them of their money. Out of the 'chor' pockets in the waistlines of the trousers, came cash. Out of the sleeves of shirts came cash. Out of the underwear pouches came cash.

'This was his bank,' said Jende. 'In the dirty clothes?'

'Maybe people don't like to touch dirty clothes,' said Peter. He realized he didn't either. His fingers were feeling grubby.

At the end, it was not an inconsiderable sum, about a bank clerk's monthly salary.

'So what should we do with this?'

'I don't know,' said Jende. 'I should take it as evidence. But I don't know evidence of what and then who knows when they will get it back. Or if they will get it back.'

'Will they want it?'

'Why not?'

'I don't know. I was just thinking: maybe they'll think it's tainted...like it's *haraam ki kamaai*.'

'You think they knew he was doing *dhanda*?'

Dhanda: cop-speak for sex work.

'What else could they think? He goes out in the night, all dressed up, comes back in the morning and he has cash now...'

'Many people don't think. *Yeda ban-ke peda khao*.'

Peter loved the phrase immediately. He tried to translate it in his head—'Act mad and eat the sweets'—and rejected it immediately. The meaning was more complex: if you did not act intelligent, you might benefit greatly. Or in this case, if you pretended to be stupid, you could enjoy the fruits of your stupidity. Ask where the money had come from and you might have to acknowledge what a beloved son or grandson was doing to earn it.

Jende rooted around and found an envelope and shoved the money in and stuck it under the shrine that contained all manner of gods and goddesses and god-persons in an eclectic mix of divinity and grace.

'No Bahuchara Mata,' said Jende.

'Who?' Peter asked.

'The goddess of the hijras.'

'He wasn't a hijra.'

Jende shrugged. Peter wanted to sigh but could not. In Jende's world anyone who was not heterosexual could be lumped into one category and it did not matter what name you gave them.

Underneath one of the figurines, there was a newspaper clipping. As by habit, he pulled it out and began reading. The headline was: 'No Time to Die'. It began with the usual graf:

The death of 24-year-old Sooraj Patel raises some issues that our society is unwilling to face. Why would a young man, recently married, in good health, choose to end his life by jumping from the eleventh-floor home in a somewhat posh Andheri neighbourhood? His mother-in-law had succumbed to organ failure at the Badama Hospital, true, and his wife did suggest that he had been overcome by grief. He left behind a note that was succinct and tragic in its brevity: 'I am sorry. It is my fault. Please forgive me' was all it said.

But why is no one outraged at the fact that this is the...

Peter ran an experienced eye over the clipping. There was no real reporting here, just the recycling of other news and some gratuitous opinion about the wastefulness of suicide and the lack of an appropriate governmental response. It ended with a comment on the need for helplines, not just Childline's 1098, but then asked a rather inane question. If the government saw the attempt to suicide as a crime, could it set up a helpline for someone planning a crime? Peter saw this for what it was: a clumsy attempt to implicate the Indian state's attitude to suicide. But it was a bad question. The State was within its rights to help people not to commit crimes; it was the definition of suicide as a crime that was the problem.

It was what the writers called 'a think piece' and what the desk called 'a chink piece': it filled a chink left in the page. 'Do they not think when they report?' Chandramouli, his colleague on the desk, had once asked sarcastically.

Jende had exhausted the possibilities of the room and was ready to leave.

'What are you looking at *raddi* paper for?' he asked impatiently.

Peter showed it to him. 'Why did he keep it?'

Jende wasn't interested. 'Who knows? Maybe he knew someone who was interviewed in it.'

No one had been interviewed. Peter could tell that. No quotation marks like tiny horns anywhere in the piece.

'Do you know the writer?'

Like most outsiders, Jende laboured under the belief that anyone who was a journalist knew every other journalist. Peter shook his head.

Jende took the paper from his hand. 'Arre, you think it's important because it came from your old newspaper,' he said.

'It's the only piece of newsprint in the entire room.'

'People keep paper for other reasons, Pittr. In my house, you will find paper under the *moortis* in the pooja corner, and under the masala *dabbis* in the kitchen, and in the drawers and so many other places, who knows.'

'Yes, but look. He also wrote the date on it.'

In one corner of the piece was the date with an exclamation mark.

Jende shrugged and headed for the ladder. Peter noted the date, the name of the writer—Jotin Perry—and put the paper in his pocket.

~

When they got back to the police station, a junior officer came up with a sheaf of faxed papers that he proffered to Jende.

'Sir, the mobile company sent these.'

'Why give them to me?' Jende demanded.

The junior officer looked a little confused.

'What are these?' Jende asked, kind, deliberately offensively kind.

'Numbers, sir. From the dead man's phone. The last numbers he dialled.'

'Whose numbers are they?'

'The mobile phone company says it can tell us which ones are from their company but not from others.'

'So what will I do? Will I call all these numbers and see who they belong to? Does this look like my job?'

'No sir,' said the junior officer.

'Whose job it is?'

'My job.'

'So?'

The young man hurried away.

'What is your name?' Jende called after him.

'Zurale, sir,' said the young man after a moment of hesitation. Jende cast his eyes skyward as a peace offering and the younger man smiled in relief.

Peter and Jende worked their way towards Jende's table. Two familiar faces appeared again.

'What is this?' Jende asked, rude and cheerful all at once, as policemen seem to be when they are confronted by juniors. 'Special appearance?'

Pagmat and Durra grinned at this sally but it was clear that there was some strain in their faces.

'Sir, *bolaaycha hota*,' they said in Marathi.

Jende grunted: '*Bola*.'

They were silent. It was obvious that they wanted to speak to Jende alone.

'I'll go,' said Peter, 'Come by later if you can.'

~

On the way home, he called Dr Ajit Pitale who said he would be willing to see him after his rounds in the Masina Hospital.

'That should take me an hour. Do you know where Masina is?'

Peter knew that this was a Parsi institution, housed in what had once been the palatial residence of Sir David Sassoon, the Jewish shipping patriarch who had given the city the Byculla Mechanics Institute (where he had his wedding reception) and the David Sassoon Library (where he had always wanted to be a member, but for some reason he had never mustered up the courage to enter its portals). Bus number 4 Ltd was lumbering up and he jumped on. Forty-five minutes later he dropped off at Gloria Church and walked down the road to Masina Hospital.

The psychiatric ward was in the new building, a strange place, haunted by cement. You walked past a ward that was almost completely empty because it was reserved for Parsis and there weren't enough sick Parsis. And then there were the padlocks and the grills and the deadened faces of the patients in the psychiatric ward.

'The men are having their shaves now,' said a cheerful nurse.

'Oh?'

'We cannot allow them to shave themselves, na? They might do suicide with the blades,' she said. 'Come, doctor will see you now.'

Dr Ajit Pitale was a quiet middle-aged man with wispy hair and the face of a choirboy.

'A kidney taken? Is this an isolated incident?'

'He wrote the numeral 1 on the wall. In blood.'

Pitale raised an eyebrow and nodded.

'Hmm. It seems a bit odd.'

Odd? Was that an approved term in the Diagnostic and Statistical Manual of Mental Disorders?

As if to make up for this slip, Dr Pitale began to talk about fetishism and partialism, about notions of primitive tribes in ascribing to body parts certain magical abilities and the use of certain organs in cult performances, muti murder in Africa and the theories of Havelock Ellis. There was also von Krafft-Ebing and mentions of Polynesian practice and voodoo and juju...and then suddenly Dr Pitale stopped and cocked his head.

'But this is not why you are here.'

'No,' said Peter. 'It was all fascinating but...'

'You want me to say, "You are looking for a middle-aged man, Roman Catholic from Goa, with brownish teeth, brown eyes and hairy forearms." Right?'

'I don't expect you to be Sherlock Holmes.'

'What did you expect?'

'I don't know. A psychological profile?'

'That is a specialized skill. I have not been trained for it but I do not even believe much in it. But here's one way of looking at it. Our world is a struggle between the life force and the death wish, between Eros and Thanatos, if you want. We like to pretend that we are all on the side of Eros and that we affirm life over death. But we are also fascinated by death. It is the ultimate bad joke, the sad ending to which we must all head. How better to defeat death and decay than to be the bringer of death for someone else? Then *you* are death. You become the God of Death in the small world of that person. So we also have a special place in our world for those who are licensed to kill.'

'James Bond.'

'Just the most famous one. But the policeman with his gun and the infantry officer with his rifle or grenade; they're all sanctioned to kill and their efficiency in such matters is tolerated, even celebrated. But it is because their killing, it is believed, goes towards keeping the law. The murderer must free himself of the rule of this law. He steps out of it when he decides to kill. He may reason his way out of it. He may say, "Anyone in my place would do the same," or "A man must do what a man must do," and even "I don't care." But with each of these he is simply saying, "I am the most important thing there is." So first marker: a well-developed ego.'

'Are we talking about the Freudian ego here? Or the ego as in the normal use of the word?'

'Both. But I'd say great self-confidence. Or even the show of self-confidence.'

'Ah,' said Peter.

'And I would look for rage. For great rage. Someone who has felt that the world has not treated him right, especially if he believes he was one of the chosen few in some way, someone trapped in a world that is beneath him. Or her.'

Peter got up to go and then he hesitated. He knew he was going to ask a question that he didn't want to ask.

'Doctor...?'

'Yes?'

'Is it possible, would it be possible, for a family not to know that their son is gay?'

The doctor looked at him with clear calm eyes.

'Yes,' he said, without equivocation and gestured to the chair. But Peter felt he had said enough, he had done enough damage. He went on out, past the nurse and past the freshly shaved chins.

~

At dinner, Peter decided that he was going to have a drink. He opened the bottle of RC and poured himself a drink.

'I'll have one too,' said Millie.

'There's no wine,' said Peter.

'I'll have what you're having,' she said

'You don't normally drink whisky,' he said.

'You don't normally drink alone,' she countered. He smiled, acknowledging a hit.

'Put some orange in it?'

'That fizzy rubbish? I'll burp all night.'

He poured her a stiff one and she took it without comment. Before he had raised his glass to hers, she had knocked it off. She grimaced but said nothing more than: 'I'm off to bed. Don't disturb me if that policeman comes knocking. As if he doesn't have his own home.'

There was no malice in this, just an old habit. But he was relieved when Jende whistled long and low instead of ringing the bell. He opened the door.

'Millie-bhagat?' Jende asked in a whisper.

Peter mimed sleep and they stepped into the veranda.

'You've been drinking?' Jende asked.

'You want one?'

'No.'

They stood in silence for a while. Jende lit one of the few cigarettes he allowed himself over the course of a day and leaned on his forearms, the better to blow smoke out into the world. Millie hated the smell of smoke. Peter wasn't mad about it either but decades spent in a newsroom had inured him to it. It was only towards the end of his life that the no smoking rules had come into force.

'What did your "special appearance" want?'

Jende looked at him thoughtfully as if deciding something. Then he said: 'They wanted to tell me that their phone numbers might appear on the deceased's mobile list.'

'*Arre wah*!' said Peter.

'That's what I thought,' said Jende. 'You know why?'

'Why?'

'Because he was the personal trainer of both their wives.'

'Their wives have personal trainers?'

'That's what I was thinking. But no use checking. This kind of story you only tell when you have made it clear with the wife that she had a personal trainer whose name was L.S. Parthusta.'

'You don't believe them?'

'I believe everybody. I believe nobody.'

'But was he a personal trainer in the first place? How would he have the energy to go and train people and spend the night in a toilet?'

'Pittr. What am I saying? I don't know.'

'There must be some other relationship between them. Otherwise why would they have told you about this?'

'Standard procedure. You have to tell if you're involved. And always better to tell before rather than let someone find out and come to ask you.'

'Do their wives look like they are the kind to have personal trainers?'

Jende shrugged. Peter wondered whether his friend was bound by some kind of code of loyalty, like the blue wall of silence that the American cops are said to put up. He tried another tack.

'What about the other numbers on his phone? Maybe he'd have some clients.'

'One-by-one we're checking the numbers. But you can't call people in the night. Some even put their phones off. But so far all numbers dialled have been cancelled and getting those names is even more difficult. We have to get a court order separately for that.'

Jende's phone rang. He showed it to Peter without a comment.

'Zurale? Why is he calling you?'

'I gave him a punishment posting. To check the CCTV and mobile numbers and to find all this boy's associates. He must have found someone.'

Four

Zurale had come through splendidly. He had found an associate and had even brought him to the police station.

'He's sitting in there. Calls himself Unit,' he said. Jende grunted.

Peter got the impression of a young man, mid-twenties, trying hard to look younger. His hair was gelled and there was an earring in one ear. He had a scar on his temple that intersected his eyebrow so that no hair grew there. His clothes were very tight. His eyes were red, as if he had been weeping.

Jende went through the usual name and age and address and then arrived at the boy's work. He did not ask him what he did, he asked him what his dhanda was, his tone suggesting contempt.

'Sir, I am a personal trainer,' the boy said, trying for a little dignity.

'And massager?'

'I give sports massage.'

'Do you give *kela* massage?'

'Sir, why are you talking like that?'

'Shut up. I am not interested in locking you up even if that is what you do. I am interested in this one, your friend.' Jende held up a photograph of the murdered man, a close up of the face, peaceful in death.

The young man looked at the picture, unblinking.

'Proxy?'

'Proxy. Unit. What names you all have.'

'When we were in junior college, he would take one rupee to give proxy for students.'

'What is this "give proxy"?'

Unit grew expansive. 'Mark attendance in class. In Parel College, the teacher didn't call out the names. There's one sheet with all the names which is passed around and you sign. Proxy would sign for those students who were bunking.'

Peter wanted to know how the name Unit had come about but knew better than to interrupt.

'From that time you two are like this?'

'I, sir? I only signed sometimes, when there were too many proxies.'

'Too many?'

'Means if the paper stopped too long at one desk the teacher might get suspicious, na?' Unit said.

'Suspicious. I'm beginning to feel suspicious about you.'

'Me? Sir, why, sir?'

'Because you are not telling us everything.'

'Sir, you ask, sir. Anything you ask and I'll tell.'

'Where were you on Sunday night?'

'I was in Pune for my cousin's wedding.'

'Do you have proof of this?'

'Sir, I can bring the video and show you.'

'What is your association with the deceased?'

'He's my friend from school.'

'What was his work?'

'*You* must know, sir?'

And for the first time a trace of insolence appeared in the boy's voice.

'I must know? *I* must know? Why must I know?'

Unit stared at Jende as if he were about to say something and then he backtracked and reached for the compliment.

'Sir, you are from the police, sir. You know everything.'

'Everyone says this, right?' Jende asked Peter.

'Right,' said Peter obligingly.

'Then why do the police ask anyone anything? Why do we not just take people like this'—and here he waved a hand at Unit—'and throw them into jail? Why ask questions? Why investigate?'

'Because that is your job, sir?' Unit said, feeling his way carefully.

'Now *he* will tell me my job,' said Jende to the air. 'But he is right. I do my job. Now tell me your friend's job.'

'I do not know, sir.'

'How is this possible? You say he is your friend?'

'Yes, sir.'

'Then he will tell you what he is doing, no?'

'Sir, I do not know.'

'Then tell me what you know.'

'My friend is dead, sir,' and Peter heard a sudden break in his voice. But the boy picked up a plastic bottle of water and poured some into his mouth, holding it at a respectable distance from his lips. He took his time drinking. When he put the bottle down again, he seemed to have recovered his composure.

'I know your friend is dead,' Jende said. 'I want to find out who killed him.'

'You find him sir and leave me with him for half an hour,' Unit said and his voice was filled with a cold rage. Peter could see that Jende was surprised by this.

'Then why won't you help me?'

'How can I help you, sir?'

'Answer my questions.'

Unit scraped at the scar on his forehead. Peter smelled a genuine conflict: the desire to help at war with something else. Fear?

'What happened?' Jende asked, pointing to the scar.

'I fell. In childhood. While playing.'

It looked too fresh to be a childhood scar.

'It looks like you were in a fight.'

'How can I fight, sir? You get into trouble if you fight. You have to have connections, sir, even to fight,' he said. 'The right connections.'

Again there was the suggestion that he was implying something, a suggestion so slight Peter later wondered if he had imagined it.

Several other dead-ends came and went but Jende went at the interrogation like a dog with a bone. He got the story out of Unit, one phrase at a time. Proxy and Unit had grown up in Dadar in one of the chawls that lined the railway tracks. They had both gone to the same municipal school and the same college where they had both left after the twelfth standard.

'Why?'

'Financial problems, sir.'

Later, they had joined the Padma School of Personal Training in Prabhadevi where they had both earned their diplomas. Then they had parted ways.

'I got busy, sir. Personal training means go here, go there, come this time, come that time. Client is busy this week, wants a change. Some other client wants another change. There is no time, sir, for anything but work.'

He said this with an air of moral superiority.

'But this boy, this Proxy, he wasn't doing personal training.'

'I don't think so.'

Again the feeling that Unit was walking warily, that he wanted to say much but was choosing to say little.

'Why don't you think so?'

'Means he's not asking for clients, he's not giving any clients, he would not talk about his clients.'

'He took money from you?'

'No, he never asked for money.'

'If he did not ask his friends for money, he was making money.'

'I think so. He was.'

'Then how was he making the money?'

'Sir, why are you asking me, sir?'

'Because your number is on his mobile.'

'Sir, he is my friend.'

They went around again and again, not getting much further. Peter saw what Jende was doing. He believed in talking, endlessly talking to the suspect.

'Because they want to tell you,' he had told Peter once. 'They want to tell you everything. You remember Batli?'

Batli was a classmate with light fingers. He stole as if by reflex. If there was something that could be taken, Batli would take it. He stole books from Victoria Circulating Library that he did not want. He stole fruit from Gopi Tank Market and Kapad Bazaar that he would not eat. He stole pencils from Punjabi Book Store that he would not use.

'What did Batli like to do?'

'Steal?'

'More than stealing?'

'I don't know.'

'He liked to tell. He liked to show what he had robbed. He didn't steal and hide. He wanted to show everyone how smart he had been. All criminals are like that. They want to tell. They want to show. You only have to find the right questions.'

There seemed to be no right questions with Unit. At some point, Peter tired of the whole thing and went home. He could not help feeling that they had missed something, something that the boy had wanted to tell them. He tried to locate what this might have been but it would not come back. Just the uneasy feeling that they had missed their cue.

He crawled into bed and slept dreamlessly for the rest of the night.

~

It was past seven when he awoke. Too late for his walk. He checked his phone, but there were no missed calls from Sunil, no messages. Perhaps he had sent an email? But if he had, Millie would have seen it. She was at the computer by the window, drinking her tea, staring at the screen. Peter thought of spending the morning with her, to distract her, if nothing else, and going in the afternoon to the offices of Hindustan Book House, where he freelanced occasionally as an editor.

But by the time he had bathed and finished his breakfast of poha and a banana, he had changed his mind. He decided to take the train to his old newspaper and talk to a certain Jotin Perry, who had written a think piece on suicide.

Peter knew better than to try and find Perry directly. He knew only too well that reporters and journalists hated being asked questions about a story they had finished with. Such queries were almost always bad news: complaints; someone who wanted to say that an error of fact had been made or that the attitude taken was contrary to public interest. Reporters only wanted to meet people who could give them tomorrow's story.

And so Peter went in search of the editor who was an old comrade-in-arms and was willing to humour Peter in return for his promise to come in and do a workshop on sub-editing skills.

Jotin Perry turned out to be a young fellow with a carefully devised look of being harried by the many demands on his time and expertise. His hair was in disarray, as if he had run his fingers through it many times. Only the right sleeve of his shirt was rolled up, and his shirt was pulled out of his trousers just enough. He gave the impression that he was doing everyone involved a huge favour by leaving his desk.

'This story that you did on the suicide,' Peter began.

'What of it?'

More flies with honey than with vinegar, Peter reminded himself.

'It's such a powerful piece,' he said now, 'so cogently argued that I was wondering: is there a personal angle?'

This was pushing it but luckily Jotin Perry did not see it as a way of asking whether he had tried to end his own life. He preened just a little and then announced that he lived next to the woman whose husband had died.

'That man happens to be my neighbour,' he said.

'That's a piece of good luck.'

'You think? I call it being ready.'

When he left, Peter looked at the editor who looked at him and sighed. He picked up the phone and got the address from the Human Resources Department.

'You know this is probably illegal?' he said.

'I know. I owe you,' said Peter.

'Big time,' said the editor. 'That workshop? You'll do it free.'

'Done,' said Peter.

It was better than trying to follow Jotin Perry home.

Five

He was on his way to Andheri in a train when Jende called.

'Come,' he said.

There was something in his voice that made Peter get off the train at Bandra and head straight back to Mahim.

'Sit,' said Jende. 'Tea? Coffee? Something cold?'

There was an awful formality to the Inspector's voice.

'Trouble,' thought Peter, 'I'm in trouble.' He was immediately ashamed of himself. This was the standard knee-jerk response to the police. He tried to quell his fright-and-flight reaction.

'No trouble. Sorry, I meant, please don't trouble,' said Peter. Then to hurry things on, he said: 'Say.' He was aware of the bareness of this and opened his mouth to add something but he couldn't think what.

'You are my friend. Millie-tai is also...'

Jende shrugged to indicate that he was aware that while Millie fell short of being a fond brother's or friend's wife, a *bhabhi* in the way Bollywood's scriptwriters represented the species, she had her place in the scheme of things.

'And Sunil...' he added.

Peter's heart froze.

'For small matters, we can do something,' Jende said. 'But this is a big matter. This is murder.'

Peter could take it no longer.

'Sunil...he's not...?'

Jende looked confused.

'Sorry? What?'

'Sunil's not hurt?'

'Hurt? No. One minute, one minute. What is it you're thinking?'

'He's not been home. He's not been in touch. I thought he might be...'

Jende's face went expressionless and Peter learned another lesson in physiognomy. You might think friends did not show much expression but when they chose to clear their faces of all indicators, you saw another face entirely. This was a familiar face, one he'd seen across decades, but this was the first time he was confronted with the professional Jende. He could see why this would be a useful skill. With no expression on one face, the other face in a conversation would fill with emotion. It was the same way with interviews; if you used silence as a tool, it could provoke potent comments simply out of the other person's desire to fill the void.

'Not in touch? Out of town? Since when?'

Once again, there was no disbelief in Jende's tone. But there was nothing else either and so the disbelief was apparent.

'I don't know,' said Peter and wished this did not sound so lame. 'Well, he was in town on Sunday.'

'And this you know how?'

'There was that demonstration.'

'What demonstration?'

'Against Section 377.'

Jende's face became a zen garden of receptive inexpressiveness.

'Achha? He was there? He told you?'

'Tell *us*?'

'They are like that,' Jende said, father to father, but there was a touch of professional commiseration in his manner. He's playing me, he's playing good cop, thought Peter.

'I saw his photograph in the newspaper.'

'Ah,' said Jende. 'After that?'

'Nothing.'

'He does this often?'

'I don't know. Yes. Often. Most of the time,' said Peter, miserably aware that he sounded confused.

Jende gave him a moment and then said: 'Which one?'

Peter tried to collect his thoughts.

'Most of the time I know where he is. But sometimes he takes off. To help someone with a project. Or he'll go to a village. Or he'll be at a friend's home, overnight.'

'Just like that?'

By which Peter understood Jende to mean: doesn't he need to ask your permission?

There had been pitched battles over this. Sunil maintained that he was an adult. Millie agreed and said that adults had responsibilities and these included informing those whom they loved and those who loved them about their whereabouts.

'And when-abouts and why-abouts and who-abouts and what-abouts.'

'Don't talk nonsense, Sunil,' Millie had said. 'I don't ask all the details.'

A temporary truce had been declared after Sunil agreed to share his timetable with them and granted them the right to call if he had been out of touch for an unreasonable amount of time.

'Only who is to say what a reasonable amount of time is...'

'If you are going to be two or three hours later than the time we expect you.'

'What time do you expect me?'

'How can we expect you when you turn up whenever you want?'

'That is exactly like giving me a curfew.'

It went on and on. The result was that Sunil did try for a while to keep his parents informed but he was the kind of person who got involved immediately. He could not hear about an injustice and wait until the morrow; he would go to the library right away to build a backgrounder; he would sit down to edit something on the spot; he would join the ad hoc fact-finding mission immediately. And then all else faded.

One particular battle—when Sunil had turned vegetarian for the sake of the environment—had ended with Sunil silent and withdrawn for days, never rude but not communicating anything more than the obvious either. Millie had turned to Peter and shouted, 'You spoiled him.'

'Thank you. If that's called spoiled, I'd hope others would spoil their children too.'

Millie had looked pleased and horrified at the same time.

Peter was thinking if he even needed to tell Shiva all this, to even bother, because Shiva would know, being a father himself and his friend, when, suddenly, something else occurred to him.

'Shiva, if he's all right, why are you asking about Sunil?'

'One of the numbers on the phone? Sunil's.'

'Sunil's number? On Proxy's phone?'

That picture in the papers.

Millie's grandchildren.

Proxy in his own blood, missing a kidney.

And Sunil out of touch.

Darkness.

Darkness all around.

He found himself praying, 'It's okay if he's gay. I promise. It doesn't make a difference. But I don't want him mixed up in all this.'

Out of the fog came Jende's voice: 'You will tell us when he turns up?'

'I will.'

And Peter realized one more thing. He could no longer be part of the investigation. It would represent a conflict of interest.

'And if you...' he said, looking at Jende. But he could not bring himself to complete what he was going to say because he did not know what it was. Jende seemed to know.

'I will,' he said and his voice was suddenly the voice of a friend again.

Cheered slightly by this, Peter stepped out into the afternoon. Sunil was involved? How? Did he know Proxy? Had he been blackmailed by him? Had he...? Peter resolutely thrust the thought aside. Whatever the boy had meant to his son, there was now a connection between him and the young man in the toilet, a connection he would give anything to deny, a connection that ran through toilets and murder and missing body parts. But it was now all the more important that he follow this thread into the labyrinth. He would have to find out...what?

'When in doubt, find everything out,' he remembered Chandramouli saying. That was what he would do. He would simply follow whatever leads he could, regardless of how little they might seem to mean. Perhaps that piece of newspaper meant nothing. He did not even know if that had been the boy's handwriting in the margin, there being no samples to compare. Perhaps it was only a mistake, an accident that it had turned up in the dead boy's room. But it had been there and he could no longer let it go. He would go to Andheri and see whether he could find the suicide case. It did not matter now whether it was a dead end; he needed activity. He realized, when he stopped walking and stood at a red light to cross the road, that his legs were shaking.

~

The housing society where Jotin Perry lived was guarded by the usual bunch of hired hands, men wearing strange uniforms in blue and black with cravats that sported red-and-black stripes. Peter filled in Jotin Perry's name and flat number and held his breath. Sometimes the guards called up to see if all was kosher. But this one didn't.

He was in. There were eight buildings in all, arranged around an octagonal park, at the centre of which was a small swimming pool, blue, unreal, empty, its water glittering in the afternoon sunlight. There were a couple of old men sitting in the park and chatting. He went and sat near them. After some minutes of deliberately ignoring him, one of them decided to use the prerogatives of the elderly and simply said, '*Kyon bhai*, who are you?'

'I have come to meet Jotin Perry,' Peter said, deciding on English. It made one less suspect as a visitor in gated middle-class communities. He was about to add that he had been asked to wait a while or some such lie but the man did not seem to notice that he wasn't meeting Jotin Perry but sitting in the garden.

'*Haan*, that boy. He is a stupid. I told him about how the *zopadpatti* is stealing electricity and I told him to make an article but he is telling that this is not a story. If robbery is not a story, then what is a story?'

'Suicide?' Peter suggested. 'They like to put that kind of thing in the papers these days.'

The old man looked at him sharply. He was not going to take the bait.

'Only rape, murder, suicide and who-knows-what. Only for all that they get time.'

Fortunately the other old man was not so canny. 'We also had a suicide,' he said. 'From the eleventh floor. Over there.'

He pointed.

Peter pulled his ears and stuck out his tongue. It was

something he had seen men do when confronted with bad news. He did not know what it meant but it seemed to be the thing to do.

'That is your friend's flat, see? And next to it is the flat from which the man jumped.'

'He was depruss,' said the first old man.

'Who lives there now?' Peter asked.

'Who will live when a man is dead? His widow, Himali,' said the second old man.

'Widow-shidow,' the first man said in a tone that suggested he had other information. 'Have you ever seen her in white?'

'Thakur, what are you saying? This is twenty-first century.'

'I only say: show your marriage licence and then I will believe. Otherwise these renters, they make stories: I am married, this is my husband, this is my brother, and who knows what all they are doing. But I don't talk behind people's back like some people. I say it on the face. I say it at the society meeting, you know it...'

Peter rummaged in his trouser pockets and pulled out his phone and put it to his ear and said, 'Yes, yes, coming, coming,' and made good his escape. They did not seem to notice his going.

One of the four doors on the eleventh floor had a white sheet of paper stuck on it. Someone had inscribed the name Patel in three scripts: Roman, Devanagri and Gujarati. The door was opened by a stunningly pretty young woman, liquid eyes in a sandalwood face. She did not so much look at him as scan him, from head to toe.

'Haan?'

'Mrs Patel?'

'You are?'

'I am Peter Fernandes. I've come about the man who jumped from the balcony,' he said, before he could stop himself.

'Offho,' said the young woman and made to close the door.

'I am sorry to disturb you,' said Peter. 'But you are famous.'

The gambit worked.

'What are you saying?' she said.

'I would like to write about you.'

'Means, you're a reporter?' Her body was still barring his path but she was listening.

'Yes.' He crossed his fingers behind his back.

'So many reporters are coming. They are all wanting to talk about him and why he jumped,' she said, almost as a complaint.

'I know,' Peter said, working frantically to keep ahead of himself. 'I think they are stupid. It is you we should write about.'

'Why?'

The door was opening slightly.

'Can I have a glass of water?' Peter asked, summoning up half-forgotten lessons in sociology. He remembered something about how you had to ask for a small favour and once that was granted then it was much more difficult to refuse a bigger favour. She went off to get the water and he debated stepping into the house but decided against it. She might feel invaded and react badly. He stayed put and when she brought the water he drank it thirstily.

'Thank you so much,' he said, overdoing the gratitude.

'You can come in.' she said. So it did work, he thought triumphantly. And people said a humanities education was useless in the real world.

She led the way into a room crowded with the appurtenances of middle-class living: a sofa set in rexine with matching armchairs, a television in pride of place, a dining table with four chairs grouped conspiratorially around it.

He chose an armchair and sat down. Himali returned with another glass of water balanced on a saucer.

'So?'

'I want to know everything about you,' he said and then gave up any attempt to tell the truth. 'I want to write a piece on you for a woman's magazine. *Marie Chanelle*, it's new, set up by a French media group. You are fascinating and beautiful and if we have the right photographs, you might even make the cover.'

He wondered if he were laying it on too thick but it worked.

'See, I have always told people I am willing to do modelling but only from chin up. Understand? No *nangi* pictures, nothing like that. I come from a decent family. I have some standing. These people say *vidhva-bidhva* but they are not understanding that I am an innocent widow. But how to tell them? Is it their business? Are they coming with proposals?'

None of this made much sense to Peter. But he nodded: 'That is true. I completely understand.'

These seemed to be the right sounds, for Himali said, 'Wait. I will make some tea.'

And she vanished again. Peter relaxed. He was home safe. Himali came back with a tray on which were loaded small bowls of khakhra, fafda, chivda and two besan laddoos in their own separate saucer. In the background, the smell of elaichi-scented tea wafted from the kitchen.

'Sorry,' she said with a faintly self-congratulatory air. 'There was nothing in the house. If I knew you are coming, I could have made something.'

'You're joking?' said Peter. 'This is a feast.'

'Arre, you don't know our hospitality then. But we are in mourning, no? It was double tragedy. First Maaji died and you can imagine how everyone was feeling.'

'Were you close?'

'Family must be close, no? Even today my brother is affected so much. And I am also.' The last was said as an afterthought and, for some reason, in English.

'Your mother and brother were very close?'

She rolled her eyes.

'Close? I was telling him: get married. You are married to your mother.'

Then she seemed to feel she had said too much.

'Anyway, who is not like that. Indian men are like that, na? This one,' she said and once more she inflected it delicately to indicate that she meant her husband, 'was also like that. His mother died young so he also became her *bhakt*. I would say, sit and do puja for her, leave me to die. Then my mother became a substitute mother for him. Only I was the outsider, first there then here.'

Once again, she tried to collect herself, to withdraw from her role as a martyr to the two men in her life and their Oedipal complex.

'But in the end, I didn't die. He jumped, na? Out of that balcony. But why talk of all these things? Tell me about the modelling shoot. They say now you don't have to wear your own clothes. Like there are sponsorers and they give the clothes. Is it true?'

'Yes,' said Peter. 'Some big fashion brands.'

Her face lit up. Then she masked it. 'Arre, you're not eating? Wait, the chai will be ready.'

And she was off again.

'So what happened?' he said when she returned with the tea.

'What is there to tell? Maaji was ill and then she died. But he could not bear it because it was his fault.'

'Why?'

'Means he thought it was his fault that she died.' This came out in a rush.

'Why?'

'What do I know? See, you are asking questions about him again.'

'No, no, this is only background.'

'How much background do you want?'

'Your mother died, you were saying, and your husband felt...'

'Depressed. He was feeling depressed. He was depressed. So he took his own life. And I was left alone in this world. I will not wear western style clothes. I think I am a typical beauty, like Aishwarya Rai.'

'This is what I thought when I saw you,' he said. 'You must be finding life difficult now. How do you manage?'

'My brother helps. But I can't stay for long here. The rent is too high. My husband was in a foreign bank, now he is no more.'

'When did you get married?'

'One year two months. He was very decent. Anything I wanted, I got. But in that whole time, he did not touch me. I don't know why. I thought he was not able to do anything. So I am an innocent widow. You must mention that. People believe if they read things in the papers.'

'Perhaps that was what caused him to become depressed.'

'*Matlab*?'

'I mean, men can become depressed because they lose their ability,' he tried to inflect the word ability with a delicate nuance and felt he had failed. But he did manage to communicate his meaning.

'No, I told you. It was not that. It was Maaji. She was like his mother, so he was depressed. I think he was also gambling-shambling because he would come very late in the night. Now tell me about this story you want to do on me.'

'I just thought I would make contact today and come back next week.'

'Do it quick, please,' she said. 'I don't know when I will have to vacate.'

~

All the way home, he debated whether to tell Millie about the new development or not. There was a side of him that did not want her burdened. But there was another side that knew she would not forgive him if he did not tell her something that concerned her son.

As it was, she took one look at his face and knew something was wrong.

'What is it?' she asked.

He took a deep breath.

'That murder...'

Her face relaxed and once more he was tempted to spare her. But he knew he had to do it.

'Sunil's number is on that boy's phone.'

Her face went tight.

'It may not mean anything...' he began.

She looked at him steadily.

'It means something, Peter. It means he knows this boy. It means he is mixed up with a murder.'

'I know.'

She turned away to keep her hands occupied, moving things around in the kitchen pointlessly. He sat down on the stool by the door and tried to speak but no words would come. She picked up a tea cup and pointed it at him. He nodded.

'Don't worry,' he said as he drank.

'I won't worry on one condition: you stop worrying,' she said crisply. He acknowledged the hit with a grimace. Easier to say than to do.

'I'm sure there's some explanation,' he said.

'There is,' she said, finishing her tea. 'This is Sunil. He

is not a murderer. He may be homosexual but he's not a murderer. Let him come home and we'll find out.'

'I wish he were here,' he said.

'He will be soon and we will ask him,' she said.

Somewhere he felt a relaxing. They could handle this together. She smiled too and put her arms around him. He let himself lean on her a little.

~

That night, as they ate dinner, Millie's cellphone beeped. She glanced at it and was immediately electrified.

'It's Sunil.'

Relief flooded him.

'SMS.'

'Read it,' he said.

'Back soon. May b no range where m going.' She looked up. 'Means where I'm going, no?'

'I think so. Call him,' he said but she was already dialing.

'No reply,' she said.

But Peter was already tasting his food again and Millie's face relaxed from its rictus of worry. He was in touch. Sunil was in touch. He was not in hiding. He was not on the run.

'I'm going to church,' she said when they had finished.

'Now?'

'I'll join the vigil at Prarthnalaya,' she said.

Prarthnalaya at Bandra was one of the few places open through the night to anyone who wanted to sneak a prayer. Nuns knelt in prayer, taking turns to keep vigil in front of the Blessed Sacrament. In moments of worry, in moments of gratitude, this was where Millie went.

'All right,' he said.

'Coming?' she asked.

'No,' he said.

'Okay,' she said. 'But don't sit around worrying about

Sunil's number on that mobile. He has all kinds of numbers, that boy. He knows all kinds of people. Remember when he brought that monkey man home to interview him?'

Peter did. The monkey had been quiet and well-behaved, as if cowed by his new surroundings but she had accepted a banana from Millie and eaten it with delicate greed as Sunil and the monkey man discussed animal rights.

Millie patted his cheek and was gone. The house shrank around him and the old Konkani phrase sprang into his mind: Now the walls come to bite me. Or eat me? Once again, as often before, he regretted the loss of a language he had known so well as a boy.

The sea, he thought. The sea will help. When he left the house, he found his body moving towards Matunga Road Station instead, in the opposite direction.

He checked himself. Returning to the scene of the crime would not help.

The sea. He had ignored it too long, though his walks took him so close, just a block away, as he went down Cadell Road, almost every day.

Two days ago...no, one day ago, his life had been...What had his life been? The sum of his habits. The same habits that made him walk around Shivaji Park clockwise because that was how he took his constitutional. The park was dark now, but its edges were bright with bursts of Marathi and lycra-limned bodies. As he walked, he acknowledged that even two days ago his life had been imperfect—he would walk here worrying about the damp patch on the ceiling and having to go and talk to the neighbours, worrying about the taxes that had to be filed even though there was not much income; he had had worries even then. But they were minor worries. His life had been pretty much the way he wanted it. Meanwhile, Providence had been shaping his ends, rough-hew them how he might...

'What is worrying you, Peter?' he asked himself now, in the tone of an officious but helpful friend.

'I am worried that my son seems to be involved in a murder. I am terrified that his absence means that he is in some way more than involved. I am also worried that he might be gay.'

'What can you do about any of this?' Peter the Officious asked.

'Oh don't give me that shit,' Peter the Worried snapped. 'I know the one that goes "Give me the courage to change the things I can" and whatnot. I can't do anything about anything. If Sunil has killed someone—there, I said it, I've faced it and it doesn't feel better, in fact, I feel worse because I feel guilty now. Satisfied? Well, anyway, if that is the case, he needs to be back in the city as soon as possible and in Shiva's custody. Shiva will look after him. And if he's gay, there's nothing I can do about it but accept it.'

'Accept it?'

'Look, I'm not worried about that right now.'

In truth, he was not. The only surefire cure for worry is a larger worry.

Out of the darkness came a voice: '*Chacha*?'

He had crossed Cadell Road and walked to the shore, without knowing it. To the left was the Mahatma Gandhi Swimming Baths, ramparts like a fort, looming out of the darkness.

'Unit?' It took Peter a moment to emerge from the haze of worry and he looked half-distractedly into the young man's eyes as he did.

Unit held his gaze. His voice changed, turned seductive. 'What do you want *here*, Chacha?'

Peter found himself hurrying to answer: 'Evening walk,' he said. And before he could stop himself he added: 'And you?'

But he already knew. Unit was not here to help someone

get fit. He was here to sell his body. He was wearing a ludicrously tight T-shirt and equally form-fitting jeans. The physical trainer shtick was what he had offered the police. Peter felt a little foolish that he had believed it.

'*Kya* Chacha!' Unit said, embarrassed at being asked. He appeared strangely vulnerable, looking down at his feet, smiling sheepishly, and Peter was startled by a small wave of affection that rose in him for this young man who looked, for all his mean-streets confidence, like an overgrown boy. He wasn't very much older than Sunil.

'Chai?' he asked.

'Thank you, Chacha.'

Peter had a vague recollection of an Irani restaurant where conversations might be prolonged over a single cup of orange tea. Hadn't it been called Cafe Cadell? It had had a reputation of some sort, even then. But when they reached the corner, there was a bank in its place.

'Where's the Irani?' he asked a bit puzzled.

'Irani?' Unit's face caught the light of a streetlamp and Peter could see that he had lined his eyes and darkened his eyebrows with *kaajal*. This had the effect of making him look even younger, at least in Peter's eyes, for in his world it was babies who wore kaajal to keep the evil eye at bay. Only, Unit had put it on to attract the lusty eye of the stranger. But even without this illusion of youth, perhaps he was too young to remember the cafe.

'Barista,' Peter said and they crossed the road. Unit perked up considerably but when they sat down, he had set his face in sanctimonious, self-denying lines. He was going to refuse all refreshment. He had that look on his face.

Peter wondered if it might be because of the looks they had attracted as soon as they had walked in. But the glances were all aimed at him, the older man, the sugar daddy. He felt a tiny rill of anger. What if he were gay and had been interested in this young man? How was that any different from the old men who walked around with their young wives? Why should they be mocked? Was this all that civilization amounted to? That we were all so stuck in a certain way of looking at sex and age and class that anything outside it may be reviled openly? Was this why Sunil had been reluctant to reveal his leanings?

Leanings? Why can't I even talk about him without euphemisms in my head? Peter wondered sadly. Was that why he could not tell us?

'Nothing for me,' Unit was saying.

'Why?' Peter asked.

'Coffee on empty stomach is not good.'

'So eat something,' said Peter automatically.

'Chacha, I have had such a shock, how can I have an appetite?' But he was peering into the menu and deciding on a cappuccino and a chicken sandwich.

Peter picked up the menu to see whether his money would hold out. He hadn't topped his wallet up in a while and he had no plastic, except for one debit card, which was meant for emergencies. He went to the counter and found he had enough for a honey and ginger tea as well. When he had placed his order, he went back to the table where Unit was looking at him expectantly.

'So how long have you been in this line?' he asked.

'Uncle...' this time it was a protest. 'One sandwich, one coffee and anything you can ask or what?'

'Sorry,' said Peter. So one didn't ask such questions? He had thought the idea was to ask questions. But then he remembered the old press room saying: It's not what you ask but how you ask it. Maybe his question had been wrong. Time to start again.

'How long have you known Proxy?'

'*Chuddi* buddies,' said Unit with pride. 'We lived side-side in Parel. You know Aar Kwee?'

'No,' said Peter.

'Railway Quarters in Parel? Near the station?'

'Oh yes,' said Peter. Kwee for Q.

'What days we've lived.'

'Was it very tough?'

'Uncle, you don't know. One toilet, ten families. So the boys went outside.'

'Went?'

'Means when you had to go, na? Every morning, there would be *maha* rush. Everyone was lining up to go. So the boys went outside.'

Peter tried to keep up. There were few toilets so the boys, the young ones, shat outside.

'Arre-re,' he said. This was the first time he had ever spoken to someone who had had to defecate in the open. His world was narrower than he thought. No wonder you found it difficult to think of Sunil with another man, he said to himself.

'Means nothing like that,' said Unit, rejecting Peter's attempt at sympathy. 'Everyone goes, all the boys, so no one feels bad or ashamed. But one day, PT sir came. He says, why are you boys doing all this on the road, it's not right. Come to my house in the morning. I thought: how can he say that? Just like that? How can we just go? But Proxy was full daring. He went.'

'Did you also go then?'

'At first, no. But Proxy went and he said nothing is wrong, the *sundaas* is clean. He said he also got boiled water to bathe afterwards, and there was a nice soap, smelling of limes.'

Peter nodded.

'Some people said he would ask us to do bad things. Because everyone was saying that mine was big.'

His tone made it clear that he was talking about his genital endowment.

'Proxy also,' he added.

'Sorry?'

'Proxy's, Chacha, it was also big. Like mine.' Unit winked. 'Do you want to see?'

Peter forced a smile to hide his discomfort. 'No. I'm not like that.'

Unit laughed, an unpleasant sound. 'Arre Chacha, in this line, who is like that? Everyone is *not like that*. I see so many men. Some come every night. But they are not like that. They come to take photos with their eyes and go home and stick it into their wives, but they are not like that. One more baby comes out nine months later and he will also not be like that. No one says, Yes, I come every day because I need this every day. They say: I hardly come here, okay, this is just one time, just for fun, just to see what you types can do. No, Chacha, no one is *like that*. And the old men are the worst.'

Peter felt a terrible sadness at this. There was truly no place for the old in this young city.

'Where do you go with your clients?' he asked, hoping he wasn't opening the door to something he couldn't handle.

'Clients?' Unit laughed, but let it go. 'Who has place, Chacha? If they have a home, then they have family. If they don't have family, they are sharing with friends. Place is the problem, na? If you can't take off your shirt even, what is going to happen? You can't even do *chiyoon*. So most times it is hand motion.'

'So what do they do in Matunga Road Station?'

Unit's face closed up.

'Baba, that is different.' He pulled his ears to indicate a great sin that he was not willing to commit.

'Different means how?'

'What do I know?'

He slurped up his coffee and began eating with the economical speed and precision of someone who has to finish his food before it is whipped away from him. Boarding school boys ate that way, Peter thought. And those who came from very large families.

'Proxy died there,' Peter said. 'He died there because something was going on, no?'

Unit sighed theatrically and looked at his wrist-watch.

'See, I'm sitting here like the mangoes are going to jump into my lap. This way I'm not going to earn, na?'

'If you want the police to find out who killed your friend, you have to tell them what went on there.'

A genuine look of anger crossed Unit's face. He looked at Peter carefully, as if trying to discern something. Then he said, 'Uncle, so much education you have and you can't tell? I have already told you what I know.'

Then he got up and loped out.

Peter went home to bed. He did not sleep for a while but when he did, the dreams were unusually vivid. He saw acres of chiku orchards tonight, and amber lights blinking in a dark tunnel. He had never felt that his dreams yielded insight. His subconscious did not seem capable of sending him clues or even the most ordinary information about where he might have left his keys. There was only the feeling, as he slipped into or emerged from a dream, that he should pay more attention, or a different kind of attention to receive illumination.

~

He woke up oddly refreshed. It did not take very long for the feeling to evaporate. Sunil was not safe. Jende wanted to speak to him.

He made himself get out of bed and have a bath. Then, as he always did, he picked up the newspapers. But there too he was to have no surcease. The newspapers were full of the case. 'Terror in the toilets,' shrieked one. 'He cuts, he guts, is he nuts?' asked another. Normally it took Peter nearly an hour to get through the papers. He read conscientiously, as he would have liked his readers to. But today he found himself barred from the black-and-white comfort of doing one's duty, informing oneself, confronting grim reality and all the rest of it.

And then as they munched high-fibre toast, the improbable happened. Millie's phone rang. It lay by her plate and she picked it up and looked at it. Her face fell.

So it wasn't Sunil.

She decided to take the call. 'Yes?'

'Baba!' she said and now her face registered an explosion of joy.

Peter rose to his feet.

'Can't hear...'

He stayed where he was. If he took the phone and could not hear either, he would never hear the end of it.

'Where?'

She plugged her free ear with her forefinger.

'Who? What? Are you all right?'

She pressed the phone closer to her ear.

'You're what? Madly what?'

Peter clenched his fists.

'I can't hear anything, Baba. Just tell me you're all right.'

Then the call ended, for Millie took the phone away from her ear with a look of disbelief. She fiddled with the phone until she pulled up the last number.

'Where is this?'

How the hell should I know, he wanted to ask. Instead, he went to get the diary which had a list of telephone exchanges that they had never needed to consult.

'It seems to be in Nagaland.'

'Nagaland? What is he doing in Nagaland?'

Peter assumed this was a rhetorical question.

'I'll have to tell Jende.'

Peter stepped out into a sharp Bombay morning. The sonchafa was perfuming the air and the sky was an improbable postcard blue. The sun was still behind the buildings to the east and the world was a slightly better place.

Jende's face was still expressionless.

'Here,' Peter said. 'He called from this number. Landline.'

'Where is he?

'I think somewhere in Nagaland.'

'He called and you didn't ask?'

'His mother took the call.'

Jende nodded and Peter left again, on his own.

Six

He could not go home. There were two leads to follow: Andheri and the Railway Quarters. The Andheri suicide seemed too far a shot, too unreal to matter. Jende was right; he was clutching at straws. But when he got off the train at Elphinstone Road Station and averted his eyes from the line of men and boys squatting to shit by the tracks, he had no idea what he hoped to find there.

Outside the Railway Quarters, he looked for a building 'two down' and there it was. A senior citizen, dressed in the striped pyjamas and sleeved singlet which represented the uniform of the lower-middle-class retired man, was reading the papers outside.

'A teacher used to live here?' Peter asked.

The old man looked puzzled.

'Maybe he is retired now,' Peter continued.

'Pagmat? PWD?'

Pagmat? The name was familiar.

'No, not Public Works Department. He was a teacher. He taught in a school?'

'Ho, ho, he was in a school, but teacher? He was *ek-do ek-do*, PT master. That is teaching? No, we named him PWD because of the boys.'

'What boys?'

'The railway colony? Right near the tracks? It was bachelors' quarters at first. But then bachelors also get married and everyone can't get Badhwar Park, na?'

Peter agreed that Badhwar Park, the posh colony in Colaba, was not in everyone's fate.

'So a single man comes here when he is assigned quarters, he gets married and he brings his wife. He should actually tell the railways and they should give him married men's quarters, but what if they have no married men's quarters? What if they tell him to send his wife home?'

Peter nodded patiently, trying to appear interested. It was a common problem all over the country. Quarters meant for single men were used by entire families; students' accommodation in university hostels was often filled with wives, children, grandparents, whoever could be stuffed in.

'You bring a wife, and one day, there is a baby. Now there are three people where one man was supposed to live. That is all right. You can live. But what about toilet?'

Peter sighed. In this city, when someone mentioned toilets, you sighed.

'So the children come out to do.'

'Do?'

'Phurr-phurr, siss-suss. And in the same place that they do this, they also take bath.'

Peter was hanging desperately on to the line of logic.

'Sheeshee,' he said, assuming a tone of mild despair, very mild disgust. But this was not the right thing to say. The man seemed annoyed.

'Arre, but what to do? When you have to go, you have to go.'

'Ah,' said Peter.

'And boys will be boys, na?'

Boys, Peter believed, would often be animals, girls, angels, mutants, demons but he thought it politic to agree. 'Yes,' he said.

'So every day, I am standing where you are standing and what am I seeing?'

Peter took this to be a rhetorical question.

'Boys coming in the morning to his house. One day, yes. Two days, yes. Every day?'

'Why?'

'That is what I am asking. So one day I caught one boy and asked why he is coming here. I thought maybe Pagmat is running a tuition class. And what does he tell me?'

'What?'

The man took a deep breath and then said: 'He tells me they're coming to take bath.'

He raised both eyebrows.

'Oh yes, to take bath.'

He looked at Peter significantly.

'Now you go see him and see what happens when you give boys bath, see for yourself.'

'Which floor?'

'Second floor. Door on the right.'

~

I should have a cover story, Peter thought as he knocked on the door. I should have thought about it before coming. Perhaps I could have been some kind of census taker. No, not a census taker but perhaps an opinion pollster with a fake identity card. Would that have got me in? he wondered. He himself tried not to slam the door on the eager young man or woman with the clipboard who asked for 'just a few minutes of your time' and then whipped out an eight-page questionnaire...

The door swung open. A servant had opened it, a young man in faded blue shorts who turned away almost before he had identified who it was.

'*Kon?*' came a quavering voice from within. The servant

simply went back into the kitchen and rumbled something unclear from there.

'*Aat ye*,' said the voice and Peter went in. Pagmat Sir, the PT teacher, was now in a wheelchair, his body desiccated, his skin paper thin and bamboo yellow. He seemed to be held in place, literally tied to the back of his chair, by two bands of cloth, something thicker than gauze.

'You've come for the injection? Every day they send someone new. What is happening, God knows. There was one nurse, he was good, he gave smooth, no pain. Now anyone comes and anyhow they give.'

It had to be insulin. Pagmat Sir was a diabetic who needed a shot every day and could not give it to himself.

'Who you are? What you want? No money. I don't have. No food. They don't give. You want tea? Ask for tea. That they give. They will give me also. You ask so that I get.'

As if on cue, the servant appeared. He flicked a desultory cloth at a table and asked, just as perfunctorily, '*Kuchh*?'

'Chai?'

The servant's face expressed displeasure without showing a single change in any of the many muscles that controlled its movements. Peter had observed that this useful trick was at its finest among the underpaid and overworked household help of the city.

'*Sattu, maala pan*,' said the old man.

This time a look of disgust crossed the servant's face.

'*Nantar mi saaf nahin karnar*,' said the servant. He had refused to clean up after the old man. Tea was a diuretic.

'*Mi karto*,' Peter heard himself offering.

'*Ho*,' said the servant belligerently, disbelief dripping from his voice, as he flounced off into the kitchen.

'You,' said the old man, squinting at Peter. 'Who are you? Why would you do that for me? Student? Which year? Tell me the year. And the squad. If you were on a team, then I will know you. What team, tell me? Remember. You had only one PT sir. I had hundred-hundred students from fifth to tenth. All the boys in some team or the other, even if only kho-kho. No girlie boys in our school.'

Girlie boys. It seemed as if once one was made aware of something, it turned up everywhere. Ten days ago, he had not spared more than a couple of moments thinking about gay men and women, the stereotypes they suffered and the rights they were denied. He supported the idea of gay rights in general but what they must endure on a daily basis had never concerned him. But now it seemed as if they were always being mentioned and the mentions were never kind or positive. And his own son might have endured all this. Perhaps he still did, despite his courage.

'Who are you?' the old man asked again. 'So many years. So many boys. Boys to men. That was what we were doing, Making India. Making Bharat. Making Bharat *mahaan*. How to do that? With history-geography? With Wren & Martin? No, it has to be muscles. It has to be bodies. It has to be men.'

Peter thought he should tell the PT master that Indian women did most of the physical labour that went into making India a nation: the gathering of firewood, the collecting of water, the cooking of food, the sowing of seeds, the bringing up of children, the threshing of the grain, the care of the old, the cleaning and the tending. Everywhere there were women at work: on the flyovers with hods of bricks; on their haunches, out of the line of sight of office-workers, cleaning the floors; the Millies in their millions of homes, cleaning and cooking and learning Devnagari late in life so that they could take up their sons' homework, sons who vanished when they were needed most.

But he didn't want an argument with the old man; he wanted information, a clue, something. Though he wasn't sure if there would be anything at all that he would find here.

'So they must build bodies. Clean bodies,' old Pagmat was saying. 'Do you know, I also had to teach them how to wash their hands: Sing Happy Birthday two times when you're using the soap, otherwise the germs don't die.'

And then suddenly, 'Show your body.'

For a moment, Peter thought he had misheard. Could the old man really have asked...Then he understood what was wanted. He rolled up a sleeve and popped a bicep, noting rather sadly that he should pay more attention to the rack of dumbbells at the Everfit Gym ('Where fitness lives'). The instructors were always encouraging him to do weights but he resisted stubbornly. And now Pagmat, retired Physical Training teacher, could sneer at him.

'See this,' the old man said and flexed an emaciated arm. Nothing by way of muscle seemed to arise under the papery skin but he looked proudly at Peter who felt called upon to respond.

'*Wah*,' he said, aware that his voice lacked conviction.

But it seemed good enough for Pagmat. 'Sattu! Chai!' he shouted now.

'God is not making tea,' came the somewhat gnomic reply.

'God is not needed to make tea.'

'He is needed if you want water to boil at your command,' came out of the kitchen.

This had the sound of an old and well-rehearsed piece of stage business.

'Do you remember a boy called Parthusta?' Peter asked.

'One of my students was killed, I heard. This one told me.'

'This one' referred to Sattu, who had arrived with the tea. Peter took his cup and nodded. Pagmat tasted his tea and grimaced.

'Put some sugar.'

'Arre, you have sugar problem. Doctor said...'

'What do doctors know? Put some jaggery, it's good.'

'Chha! Drink what you get or you will die.'

Pagmat Sir took a sip and made a face and turned back to Peter.

'How did he die?'

'Murdered.'

'*Dishoom-dishoom*?'

'No, re,' said the servant, lingering. '*Khachack-machack*.' He slashed an imaginary knife through the air in the manner of Zorro.

'He knows everything,' said Pagmat, sarcasm dripping.

'Arre, it was in the papers. Ask me.'

'Ask *me*,' said a new voice. Peter looked up and saw the tired khaki of the police department. The servant left the room without a word and came back with tea.

'*Now* God is making tea,' said the old man.

'No. Sattu is making tea for himself as per usual. But now that I'm here, I'm lucky.'

'Kya, sahib,' Sattu said but he seemed to be asking for forgiveness rather than challenging what the policeman was saying. His demeanour had undergone a change. He was not ingratiating but he was no longer sullen either. The policeman ignored him and focussed on Peter.

'I have seen you somewhere.'

'Funny,' said Peter. 'I was going to say the same thing.'

And in the next instant, he realized that the cop had placed him.

'You are...'

Peter could see him struggling between the officious and the placatory. He decided not to wait until Pagmat Junior made up his mind. He got up and said, 'I will take your leave now. Your son has come.'

'Sit.'

Peter sat. The word was a command. So might Pagmat Senior have brought an unruly hockey team to order.

'You are not my student.'

'No.'

'Then why are you here?'

'That boy who was murdered...'

Suddenly the cop exploded.

'Who are you? Aahn? How you're coming here, telling all lies and all. Come on, get out of here.'

'Ay,' said the old man, '*Chi-bas.*'

Shut up, sit down, all rolled into two crisp Marathi syllables.

'This is my house. He will go when I tell him to go. He will stay as long as I want him to stay.'

'Kaka...'

Uncle. Of course.

The cop was not his son.

They only shared a name.

'I have been a *brahmachari* all my life. All my students know. That is why I said: you are not my student. How would I have a child?'

Peter smiled, the appreciative smile of someone who has spotted his better.

'Sorry, sir,' he said.

'Ask. What do you want?

'About that boy who was murdered.'

Pagmat Junior's eyes were fixed on him. Peter ignored him.

'He would come here often?'

'He would come here often,' old Pagmat confirmed.

'When?'

'When he was in school. To take a bath. To do potty. Those people were making their boys do potty on the roads. How can they do that? Is that clean? Is that good? So I told the boys who came to my school, come to my house, do your potty, do your bath and then go to school.'

'No one took objection to this?'

'They took. They always take. But why will that bother me? Should I bother? They would come here and take bath and go to school. Clean.'

'They must have been very grateful to you.'

'I am not doing it for gratitude. I am doing what I must do.'

'Did you keep in touch with him?'

Pagmat Junior shifted slightly, He seemed to be about to say something but then stopped himself.

'Do students keep in touch with teachers?'

'I suppose some do.'

'Are you grateful to your teachers?'

'I suppose I am. To some at least.'

'Do you keep in touch with them?'

Peter felt a lick of shame. He turned up at their funerals. As much because he was grateful to them as because it was a place to meet such school friends as still lived in the city.

'Do you know if he had any enemies?' he asked.

'Ohffo, how will I know? I have nothing better to do than to go around like that, asking about friends and enemies?'

Peter gave up. As he made his way to the door, Pagmat Junior smiled a strained smile and said, 'Sir. Sorry.' He had remembered Peter was the Inspector's friend and he had swallowed his rage. There was a hierarchy here. It was never a good idea to forget hierarchy; government taught you that much if nothing else.

'My uncle is very old, sir.'

'I can see that.'

'No need for trouble.'

'No,' said Peter.

In other words, Pagmat had not told Jende anything about his uncle's connection with the dead boy. That in itself was not surprising. No one wanted anything to do with the police; not even the police. But then why had he—and that friend of his, Durra—turned up at the scene of the crime?

No, he told himself, I'm grabbing at straws. The men must have just been passing by as they had claimed. They could not have known about it being a crime scene nor even who had been murdered. But the niggle remained and when he pushed at it, he could see Sunil hovering behind. Anything, anyone…

But that was bad policy. To want it to be Not-X, one made a case for it to be Y.

Peter thought back to Babu, the man who washed cars in Spence Lane, Nagpada, where his grandmother had lived. Babu also 'obliged' if your maid went missing and you were expecting guests and your floors had not been cleaned and your bric-a-brac had not been dusted. One day, Tehmina Mai had been expecting her scrupulous sister-in-law, the kind who would make white-glove inspections of any home she visited. She called Babu for a quick touch up. The next morning, she found a gold chain missing. The police were informed and they asked, as is their wont, who the servants were. No bai that day—'*Main toh bach gayi*,' she would later say, grabbing the lobes of her ears and casting her eyes up to heaven in gratitude for the husband who had beaten her and made it difficult to get up that morning—and so Babu was taken to the lock-up and duly confessed. Everyone had different views on his perfidy. Some said it was the demon drink; others said an open purse would tempt a saint; a very few said they found it difficult to believe. Three months later, a plumber found the chain in a choked drainpipe. Tehmina Mai went straight to the police station to say that she had made a mistake. Babu was released but he was not the same person. His spirit was broken and it became clear that his body had not escaped either. He found that there was another young man doing 'his' cars. Anyway, it was difficult now to carry the buckets of water needed to wash cars and a few weeks after his release, he vanished quietly into the delirium of a May afternoon.

Only the truth, then. Hopefully the truth. And what did Peter have to lead him to the truth?

Bits and bobs. Bits and bobs. That was all.

No pattern, no motive, nothing. Just a dead body.

The body of a young man in a railway station toilet.

The number '1' written in blood on a wall.

A physical trainer who did not train.

A well-endowed physical trainer.

No, two well-endowed physical trainers.

A young man who had sex with men for money.

Who would know about these things?

~

It was Millie who reminded him.

'Why don't you go and talk to Leslie?'

For a moment, Peter was speechless. Leslie was the open secret of Millie's family. He was a 'confirmed bachelor', an advertising man, Leslie Siqueira, wearer of silk kaftans and scarves hand-painted for him, author of a terrible camp novel from the Calcutta-based Writers' Workshop. Why hadn't he thought of him earlier?

Because he hadn't wanted to.

He did not want to think of Leslie and his son in the same...

In the same what?

He decided that it would be best not to end his own sentence.

He called Leslie and was told that Her Highness was at home to guests.

On the way to Bandra, as the train passed Matunga Road Station, Peter forced himself to think of Sunil visiting the toilet to find sex. It was distasteful. He felt a trickle of shame. How modern he had thought himself. How free of judgements. He tried another experiment: His son seeking out a woman for sex, a prosti...no, sex worker. No, why was he equating the men in the toilet with men seeking sex workers? They were not paying nor seeking to be paid there. They were only looking for something they could not have outside.

Okay, then. Sunil at a swingers' bar, looking for meaningless sex with a woman. A series of women. Still distasteful. Peter felt a moment of relief. Not so bad after all. He was only suffering from the parental inability to see one's child as a sexual being. Was that a universal thing? Or was it peculiarly Indian? Did it have something to do with being Roman Catholic? Both had always seemed like convenient explanations, not really applicable to himself and so to no one else.

But he was too honest to let himself off the hook entirely. Still distasteful, yes, but nowhere near as distasteful as the thought of his son in a gay bar.

Seven

Leslie lived, as befit someone who had once dubbed himself the Queen of the Queen of the Suburbs, in a small cottage on one of the Saint Streets in Bandra. It had a patch of garden with two trees: wild mango and palash.

The door was opened by a bright young man.

'Sorry…' Peter said, stepping back. The boy was the wrong age, the wrong look, the wrong everything. He was wearing a linen shirt and khaki trousers. Neither of these did much to cover up his gym-toned body. But there was more—an improbable perfection in the lines and angles of his limbs and face. Bewildered, Peter tried not to stare.

'Hello. You're looking for Leslie sir?' the young man asked, speaking English with a slight, deliberate American accent.

'Yes,' Peter said.

'Are you Peter Fernandes?'

'Yes.'

'He said you're coming. Please come.'

He led Peter into a living room and sat down with the air of someone who had every right to be there. Peter looked around. The Bandra bungalow was as it had always been: cool, quiet and an odd mixture of Leslie's taste and his family's love of kitsch. There were beautiful Murano blown-glass vases and an embroidered pastoral scene in which a shepherd offered a rose to a coy mermaid.

'Your name?' Peter asked.

'Himal Shah,' said the young man. Peter could not help feeling that he said it in a way that suggested it ought to be recognized.

'And what do you do?'

'I'm working right now, but I am also studying,' Himal said.

'That's good,' said Peter, feeling some answer was required. The young man was looking at him intently, expectantly, so he asked: 'What are you studying?'

'Education is one way to get ahead in this world, isn't it, Uncle?'

'It is,' Peter chose to agree.

'If you don't have expensive education, you're nothing, right?'

'I don't think...' Peter began.

'Whatever good qualities you have, how much ever you do, the world only wants to see your *papad*,' said Himal and there was bitterness in his voice.

At that moment Leslie emerged from an inner room in a kaftan of many colours, clearly dressed for the occasion. Himal rose immediately and excused himself.

'I must go to work.'

Leslie inclined his head graciously.

'Needs must when the devil drives,' he said and smiled with the air of La Gioconda.

'*Ça va*, Pumpkin Eater?'

'*Ça va bien*,' said Peter self-consciously.

'And that brings us to the end of all the French Pierre knows.'

'You got me there.'

'You wish, dear, you wish.'

Peter tried to change the subject.

'Who was the young man?' he asked. For he was still a

little disoriented by the unexpected encounter at the door. And now, thinking back, the face seemed familiar. But no, it was not the kind of face you would forget. Nor was the body. Together, they were unforgettable in their almost plastic beauty.

'The young man goes by the name Himal Shah. He's my boarder.'

'Ah,' said Peter.

'What an evil mind you have, my dear Peter,' cooed Leslie. 'I assure you I am purr-actically in loco parentis. Though when he prances through the room in just a wee towel on his way from a bath, I have such thoughts as would shock Oedipus.'

'I'm not really...'

'Besides, I never have sex with anyone who is paying me money. He's a genuine boarder. He works somewhere nearby in a laboratory of some kind.'

'He's a scientist?'

'Does he look like a scientist? I think he's a technician. Though such hours he keeps! I had no idea these lab people keep such hours. Or maybe he's a spy of some kind—except you'd spot that steaming dish from the moon. More likely a bouncer, which would explain the muscle. You did notice his thighs, didn't you? Even *you* would, and don't you frown, it frightens me.'

Leslie could never answer a question with a monosyllable.

'You've taken a boarder?'

'Does it sound very tacky? I do assure you the very best people have had boarders. Perin Gobhai in those dark years had that lovely Shai and before her there was Dr Banaji, you know the one who plucks the pearls out of your eyes. I love that phrase: *moti aana*, though cataracts is also quite ...'

This was a long road down which they would walk.

'I suppose we're all feeling the pinch,' Peter interrupted.

'Ooh, I love it when you talk naughty.'

Then he looked at Peter and cocked his head on one side and asked:

'So what can Her Highness do for you, my rock?'

'What goes on at Matunga Road Station?'

'We presume you're not talking about the way the trains come and go, humming of Michelangelo? We presume you're talking about The Scene?

'Yes.'

'Oh well, the usual, I suppose. Some Dadar boys flutter down when things get too hot at the south end of platforms two and three. Some Bandra babas hustle south when the police sweep them off platform one. And then there's the local talent. There's a college or two around and they're always ready to be taken down. Did I tell you about...?'

'Leslie.'

'Ooh, we're focussed.'

'It's a murder.'

'How fearfully thrilling. Is it the one that happened under the old stone bridge?'

'That one.'

'Oh, I could tell you some stories about that place. Some stories that would make each individual hair stand upon your head as upon the fretful porpentine. And some of your colleagues would figure too. And then there was the man with the small stones he used to knock out the lights.'

Peter sighed.

'Why is the Matunga Road Station toilet so popular with gay men?'

Leslie looked thoughtful.

'That is a question that has exercised us in the many hours we have spent in those very toilets. I think it's about placement. When the loo is out of the way, it works as a gay adda. If it's right in the middle of things, it's much more difficult to have some fun. Then the partitions should be low enough to reach over and the stalls must not be too wide so you won't be able to reach across. Indian toilet planners—can you imagine? What a phrase. Who do you think designs these things?—anyway, whoever they are, they try to maximize space, so you get narrow stalls, all cosily close.'

'Leslie.'

'Right, right. Okay, let's see. Matunga Road. Yes, it is out of the way. The police have to walk off the platform to get there and they'd rather not. There's only one row of urinals so you don't have to worry about what's going on in the other row. All the talent is lined up, as it were. By contrast, the old loo on Bandra's platform one was a nightmare, with urinals in a big square formation. Then Matunga has two entrances, both open, so you can make a quick exit if you want. Cops come in one side, you go out the other.'

'Do the cops trouble the gays much?'

'The cops trouble everyone, dear Peter. You know that. But it is my understanding that they trouble the criminals least of all. And since we are criminals according to the law, most of the time they ignore us.'

Peter smiled mechanically at this rather clumsy witticism.

'Speaking of ignoring, do you know that almost everyone in this city ignored my novel?'

Peter smiled although he didn't want to. Ignoring Leslie's novel had not been easy; he had called and phoned and written messages and sent multiple copies. If it had been ignored, it was because it was a terrible novel; nothing to do with its gay content. He wondered if somewhere Leslie knew this too.

'You'd think they'd review it to cash in on the pink rupee. Do you know, we used to say, he's as gay as a two-rupee note? Because they were so pink! Those lovely old notes. I mean, who gets to design them? I'd love to design a note myself.'

'Leslie.'

'Oh where was I?'

'The cops?'

'Oh yes. Well, the Mumbai cops would generally leave us alone. Most of them have better fish to fry, I think. But some of them, my dear! There was one who would make you do *baithaks*, up-down, on your knees—and then you had to, if you know what I mean? And another wanted vadapao. You do know what vadapao is, don't you, Peter?'

Peter didn't. But he was beginning to feel a sick fascination for Leslie's world.

'Can we get back to the cops?'

'My, we are hung up on the boys with the batons, aren't we? Let me say I've taken some lathis in my time.'

'The cops.'

'Is this the third degree?'

'I'm sorry, I could go and ask...

'Don't you dare ask anyone else. I will cast you into outer darkness where there is gnashing of teeth and wailing. What is it you want to know?'

'I don't know. Anything. Everything.'

'And yet, every time I try to talk about something, you stop me.'

Leslie suddenly looked up and turned a cool and intelligent eye on Peter.

'To give some, you have to get some. Spit it out, young Peter, or you might swallow it.'

'Okay, a young man, a personal trainer, is found murdered. He's slashed to death in a toilet.'

'I saw the papers.'

'He was very well-endowed.'

'Gracious, was he starkers-parkers?'

'No. I was told this by his friend, a masseur and rough trade, I think.'

Leslie said: 'So you want to know how this thing might have come to pass?'

'Yes.'

'Am I in possession of all the facts?' Leslie raised an eyebrow. Just one. A neat trick.

Peter decided to risk it.

'There are two policemen involved.'

'How?'

'That's the thing. I don't know.'

Leslie waited.

'They turned up at the scene of the crime.'

'Isn't that where they're supposed to be?'

'No, this wasn't their beat.'

Leslie nodded.

'No. I can't imagine any Indian turning up where he doesn't have work. And where he might suddenly get some work added to his plate. No, you're right to be suspicious. Anything else?'

'The dead boy's friend tells me I should go and talk to a teacher. A retired teacher.'

Leslie raised both eyebrows.

'This is not a case. It is a sugarcane stick: long and juicy and hard.'

'This PT teacher lives near the boys, he did when they were young at least. He lets them come and have baths in his house.'

'Ooh!'

'He's unmarried.'

'Double-ooh.'

'And his nephew is one of the cops who suddenly turns up at the scene of the crime.'

'Double-ooh seven!

'I don't know what to make of any of it.'

Leslie laughed.

'I can see that. It's so simple, Peter, it would jump out at any gay man. A toilet. A gay man. A policeman. This is why I argue for diversity. The more people there are, the more kinds of experience you have on hand to call upon and therefore the more you know.'

Peter was about to say that he knew all the arguments for diversity but he realized that this would be the wrong tack to take. He let Leslie rant on about diversity and tell tales of the number of times a gay man's special understanding of the world had saved the day at the advertising agency at which he had spent so many years of his life as an art director. This was a familiar tune and he let Leslie play it for a while. He wondered as he listened whether Leslie had any anecdotes about how someone from another marginalized section of society—an Adivasi, say, or a Dalit—had brought his or her knowledge to a problem. Then he decided this was uncharitable.

'I still can't get the connection,' he said when he had let Leslie go on as long as he thought suitable.

'What's common to Alan Turing and George Michael?' Leslie was now in Cambridge don mode, his fingers steepled.

'They're both British?'

'Ye-es?' said Leslie and his tone suggested that Peter should go beyond this commonplace.

'They're both gay?'

'And?'

The same tone.

'Okay, give up. I don't know.'

'Cottaging. A peculiar British term for looking for sex in public toilets. Turing was caught doing it, I think. He was a genius, he helped crack Enigma—the German code machine, I think—and Britain won the war, but that didn't matter at all when peace broke out. He was sentenced just the same.'

'They chemically castrated him or something like that?'

'Yes, he was arrested for soliciting. Can you imagine? In 1952, not the Dark Ages. And then he killed himself, poor dear, when he couldn't bear the shame.'

Peter began to resent Leslie's easy assumption of himself as the only one who knew anything about Turing's story.

'Didn't his mum say he wasn't suicidal and that it was some accident involving cyanide and an apple?'

'Oh his *mum*,' said Leslie. 'Parents are absolutely the last to know *anything*. My mother went to her grave sure that I was saving myself for the right girl.'

Peter almost winced. A hit, a palpable hit, he thought. But there was also a comfort in knowing that other parents lived in a cloud of unknowing.

Leslie was continuing: 'George Michael got into a spot of bother too—in Beverly Hills, of all places! But of course attitudes had changed a little by '98. He wasn't threatened with jail or with chemical castration.'

'Okay, I'm still lost. What has all this got to do with the young man who was killed?'

'In poor Turing's days, if the Brits wanted to clear up some gays and toss them in the chokie, they would choose a nice-looking young copper with a big dick and tell him to position himself in a loo and get himself an erection. Then with his dong sticking out, he had to wait until a size queen approached him, and then they'd pounce. He'd be brought up before the beak and a clear message would be sent out to all the other—what was that peculiar word they used—inverts? Yes, inverts. That would tell all the other inverts that rum, buggery and the lash might be well and good when Britannia was all at sea but on land, the hetters would have their way.'

'This boy wasn't a cop, Leslie.'

'No, he wouldn't be. He'd have been chosen for his looks. He must have been fair…No, you did tell me he was well-endowed. So it was his equipment that got him the gig. Yes, my guess would be that it would be his equipment that qualified him for this job. So there he is, at the loo at Matunga. He lines up, pulls out his dick, gives it a wiggle, thinks about something sexy, gets a stiffy and then waits until someone suitable comes along. Then when the hand sneaks across the partition and winds itself around him, the police make their move.'

'This seems like a lot of work to arrest a couple of gay men. Or even one gay man.'

'Oh no, this isn't about arrests, my poor and innocent Peter. They don't arrest the men. You should look up the records. In the hundred or more years we've had dear old Macaulay's Sec 377, it's been used about ten times, if that.'

Leslie stopped. Peter asked dutifully: 'Then what is this about?'

'It's about blackmail. You get the right man, someone middle-class, someone who looks like he's got a good job to lose, someone who doesn't want his proclivities paraded in the press, and you drag him to a police *thana*. To make things look right, you drag along the young man with the nice dong too. There you split them up in the best tradition of Prisoner's Dilemma. You take the boy into another room and you take a nice leather strap with him. The door closes and the mark hears the strap fall and he hears screams. There is no suggestion that the police will do that to him. He is not told it will be his turn next. He simply assumes it will be. He's already terrified. All his closetty life, he has feared this moment and now it is happening. He never learned to box, in fact he hated boxing so much, he couldn't bear to watch it, not even for those flirty high-cut shorts. Now he wished he had bothered, at least he'd be able to bear the pain. But he got out of it. He wants to cry but he doesn't because he knows the men in khaki already have such a low opinion of him and this will make them think he's a chhakka or a woman. He will do anything at this point to get out of there.

'And that's when they offer him a deal. The cops are saying, "We can see you're from a good home. You made a mistake. If you bring this much money"—I don't know how much the average amount is but there's a helpline at Gay Bombay and they should know. Bring that much money, they say, and it will all go away.'

'I suppose they share the profits?'

'I suppose. I don't know what the shares are but I'm guessing the men in khaki keep the lion's share and give the poor little stinker a bit of the offal. So that's the link. That's what was happening. That was what the police had to do with this little boy. He was their honey trap.'

'But why would they kill the boy?'

'Gosh. Did I say they killed the boy?'

Peter thought back.

'No.'

'My guess is you will never know who killed him. No one will care. What kind of boy would agree to this sort of job? To stand with your dick hanging out in a public loo until a man comes up to you? You know what they call these boys in New York? Gay dirt. This boy must have been someone who couldn't find any other work. He must have been poor and in this country, poor people die every day and no one cares.'

~

As Peter walked through the quiet bylanes of Bandra, he thought about the blackmail plan. How would anyone know who had a penis of the right size? In Britain, he supposed, it was the changing room and the communal showers and all the rest of that. How would an Indian man know who was 'big'?

Himal appeared around a corner.

'Sir?' he said. 'You met Leslie sir?'

'Yes, thank you.'

'He is not himself these days.'

'Really?' Peter thought back to the figure in the kaftan on the *chaise longue*. Yes, there was a bit less energy than normal but surely that had to do with old age. 'I didn't think so,' he said.

'He is not well, sir,' said the young man, inflecting his voice with grave meaningfulness. Peter frowned.

'Cancer?'

'AIDS, sir.'

Should he be telling me? Peter wondered.

As if guessing his thoughts, the young man said: 'You are his cousin-brother, Peter sir. This is why I am telling you. Because he will need your help.'

Peter frowned again.

'Sir, AIDS has effect on the brain as well. The virus invades everywhere. It makes people do funny things. It makes them say funny things also.'

Again, this was inflected in a way that suggested there was a deeper meaning but Peter was already uncomfortable.

'Well, thank you for telling me.'

He walked away and decided to call up Jende and see what he was up to. The phone rang but Jende did not answer and so he decided to take a chance on this and see where the inspector's mind was heading. He knew he would not be welcome. He knew he would be on sufferance, but he owed it to Jende to tell him what he had found out.

Or what he thought he might have found out.

Eight

Jende only looked slightly suspicious when he turned up.

'I'll make this quick,' Peter said.

'First have tea.'

So things were going back to normal, it would seem. He sat down.

'Your son?'

'He called but I could not give him your message.'

'Achha?'

And still it was not clear whether Jende believed him or not.

'The line was not clear. Anyway, I went to meet…'

And he spilled out the story of his meetings and movements but he noted even as he was saying all this that Jende's hands were not moving. He was not making notes and no notes meant he was not taking any of this seriously.

When he was done, Jende said: 'Aah.'

'And what Leslie says may explain why those cops' numbers were on Proxy's phone.'

'Aah,' said Jende again and then threw him a googly.

'You should go home,' he said.

'I know,' Peter said. 'I should not be interfering, but what if your son were involved? Would you be able to stay away?'

'No,' said Jende. 'But you should go home now. Millie-bhagat will be waiting for you.'

Peter gave up and left the police station. He could not

tell what Jende was up to or what his mood was like. But when he got home, the door was opened by a jubilant Millie.

'He's back!' she all but shouted.

Peter looked around. A rucksack was lying on the floor, wide open, used clothes spilling out of it. For a moment, he flashed back to the dead boy's home with its carefully thought-out banking system.

He sat down with a sigh.

Millie produced the newspaper and placed it at his elbow. She was about to leave the room when he gestured to her to sit down. She hesitated and sat down again.

Sunil came out in T-shirt and shorts. He sat down and looked at both of them.

'What's up with the two of you?'

Peter handed him the newspaper.

Sunil looked at it and laughed. 'God, look at Meera. She's...'

Then he stopped laughing and looked up at the two of them.

'The caption,' said Millie.

'Gay activist Sunil Fernandes...' he began to read it out and shook his head. In disbelief? Peter wondered. Then it dawned on him. 'You think...wait a minute.'

He shook his head again.

'Is there something you want to tell us, Sunil?' Peter asked.

Sunil's face hardened. Impassive, like a wall, Peter thought. Like Shiva's that day at the thana.

He waited.

'Are you asking me if I'm gay?'

'Yes,' said Peter, wondering if this homecoming could get any worse.

'I'm not going to tell you. I don't think it's anyone's business except my own.'

Peter tried to make sense of this. He had been preparing

for a 'Yes' and hoping for a 'No'. But this? And then Millie laughed as if it were the answer she had been waiting to hear.

'Yes,' she said. 'It's no one's business except yours. I'm going to get us a cup of tea.'

She went out of the room.

'That's not going to work,' said Sunil to her departing back. She turned and threw him an amused glance. Then she winked at Peter and went off. He could hear her singing a *fado* somewhat off-key.

Sunil sat there, his face a wordless snarl now, defying his father to continue with that line of questioning, marshalling, no doubt, arguments about privacy and the equality of all tastes. Peter took comfort in the fado and decided to abandon the topic.

'Jende would like a word,' he said.

'With me?'

'With you.'

'Uncle Shiva must...'

'No, it's Inspector Jende who wants a word.'

Sunil's face hardened again a little. It was a man's face, Peter realized now. A man who was drawing lines to exclude them. Had it been changing all the while, forming like a patina, each scouring of hurt, each scraping of beard removing further traces of childhood? Did he know nothing of Sunil's face because he knew so much about it?

'What is this about?'

'It's about a dead boy.'

'Boy?'

'Man, I suppose I should have said.' Peter wondered whether he had used 'boy' because the dead man was gay.

'Dad, start at the beginning.'

Peter told him the bare bones of the story.

'Proxy? Dead?'

'You know him?'

'Yes, I know him. My MPhil thesis was with high-risk people; the efficacy of NGOs that work in AIDS prevention.'

Then his voice dropped.

'He was also a friend.'

Peter thought: My son, my son. He did not even want to think about what kind of friendship they had. But would it matter if Sunil were paying Proxy? Perhaps it might if he were also relying on him as a subject for his thesis. No, he said to himself, you cannot ask. You will not ask. You must not ask. It is his life and his money and his body. He must remain our son.

'So this boy was also...uhm...selling himself?'

'I don't think you should equate sex with self, Dad. Let's just say I think he did sometimes indulge in MSM and there might have been commercial transactions involved.'

As Peter tried to decode that, Sunil added: 'Before you ask, MSM is men having sex with men.'

'That is different from gay?' Peter asked.

'It's a question of personal choice. If a man says he's gay, then he's gay. If he says he has sex with men but doesn't say he's gay, then the right term is MSM. Anyway, sexual identities can be very fluid.'

There was a moment's silence.

'Stop it, Dad.'

'Stop what?'

'Stop trying to second-guess me.'

'Wouldn't you?'

Sunil sighed.

Just then Millie came out and said, 'Your police friend wants to see him, no? Better take him and go.'

'What's the rush?' Sunil asked.

'Best to finish these things as soon as possible,' she said.

At the station Peter went in first, as if he had to interpose his body between his son and the police. Jende was at his desk.

'He's back.'

'I know.'

'You know?'

'Why do you think I told you to go home?'

'How did you know?'

'We were keeping watch on your house. How else?'

Sunil stiffened but Peter signalled that he would explain later. Jende gestured Sunil to a seat. To Peter's relief, he asked him the relevant question immediately:

'Where were you, Sunil, between ten p.m. and seven a.m. on Sunday night?'

'I was on a flight. To Delhi. I have my boarding passes if you want.'

Jende shrugged.

'Okay. Bring them later,' he said. Then he asked, 'You keep boarding passes?'

'If you travel on government money, they want to be sure you took the flight. So you attach your boarding pass when you get back.'

Jende raised his eyebrows, considering this. Peter could tell he was trying to discern the intentions of the mind that had thought up this rule. Jende thought aloud to himself, a sign that he was comfortable: 'Got it. If you have a boarding pass, you have taken the trip. Otherwise you might just buy the ticket and cancel and take the money and not go.' He nodded his approval. 'The government thinks of everything.'

Then he began his questioning but there was an odd, relaxed quality to it.

'Why is this Proxy calling you?'

'He was my friend.'

'Friend,' Jende repeated, trying to keep the exasperation out of his voice. 'How did you come to meet this friend?'

'Through an NGO I interned with.'

'Which one?'

Sunil gave him the name. Jende nodded.

'Try and keep your parents informed of where you are next time.'

Sunil smiled briefly and left. Shiva turned to Peter.

'*Chala*,' he said. 'We have work to do.'

'You really didn't want to talk to Sunil, did you?'

'No.'

'Why not?'

'Because we have his GPS records from his cellphone. He could not have killed Proxy.'

'Why didn't you tell me?'

'You thought he had killed the boy?'

This was unanswerable but Peter was filled with the desire to hit his old friend on the head with his own lathi.

Instead, he tried another tack.

'Can we talk to those cops?'

'Pagmat and Durra? Why?'

'They might have killed him also, no? Their numbers were on his phone.'

'You're mad or what?' Jende said. 'Why would they kill him? They found someone to do their dirty work. Otherwise, one of them would have to go and stand there.'

Peter took this to mean that Leslie's thesis was now acceptable to Jende.

'But suppose he planned to reveal their game?'

Jende shook his head.

'Who would believe this fellow? How would he give proof? And who would he tell? The police? And why would he do this? What would he do for money afterwards? Remember, he was also earning.'

'I suppose he could go to the press.'

'With what story? That he would go and show his thing in the toilet for policemen to earn some money? You think they would put him in the papers without his photo? How would he show his face?'

'Maybe you're right. Where are they, Pagmat and Durra?'

'Both on long leave.'

'Unpaid?'

'Enough, aahn? They should be sacked. I know. You know. Police knows. But it is difficult to prove anything so they are on long leave.'

'And they get their pay?'

'Yes. But for them it will be like not having salary.'

All over the city it was known that the police were not paid well enough. All over the city it was assumed that policemen were fabulously wealthy because of the amount of money they could make on bribes. Suddenly, Peter became aware that he was talking to one of the rare birds: an honest cop.

'How do you manage?'

'Manage?'

'Without taking bribes?'

'The wife earns,' said Jende. 'This corruption thing is too much of a headache.'

'But it must be difficult to manage.'

'What expenses do I have? Boys are in SSC school so seven rupees for seventh standard, ten rupees for tenth standard. Quarters are from police. Uniform from police. Bike from police. Fuel from police.'

He shrugged and it was clear to Peter that he was uncomfortable talking about himself.

'So what now?'

'We will have to just go and finger.'

Peter flashed back to Victoria High School and the games under the two mango trees in the quadrangle where if you wanted to finger another boy, it was not because of homoerotic intent but because you wanted to torment him. 'Don't finger, yaar,' one boy might say to another.

Something inside his stomach relaxed because he was

back in familiar territory, back with his friend, back on the right side of the law, back on the same old terms. But even as he thought this, he knew it was not true. He would never be on the same terms again. He would always remember the expressionless face and voice, that complete exclusion. When Jende had not told him that Sunil was in the clear, he had been fingering again, keeping information back so as to get as much further information as he could. So what if they were friends? This was a murder investigation. It is only when you find yourself outside that you know that there is a fence and you had once been inside it.

Nine

When Peter got home, Millie was cleaning mackerels. He could feel she had something to say so he dragged a stool over and perched on it next to her in the narrow kitchen.

'So?' she said. 'What did your friend want with Sunil?'

'No, that was cleared up. He knew the dead boy through his work.'

'I thought so.'

He watched her scoop the entrails out and rinse the empty belly of the fish under the tap.

'You know,' she said, 'when he came back and he was safe, I sat there thinking, "He may be gay" and then I thought, "So what if he is anything? It's all right. He's my son and he's safe. He's with us. What is there to cry about that?"'

Peter realized his eyes were wet. He hugged her and she also began to cry, but these were not tears of anger or pain. They were tears of relief and for a long time they stood there, body to body, his nose in her grey hair, with its familiar smells of coconut oil and mint, drawing from her the strength of a long association, the years of a common bed and a common kitchen.

Then she elbowed him affectionately out of her way.

'All this when the *baangdas* have to be fried?'

'*Reichado*?'

'What other way is there to make these smelly things?'

Millie did not like mackerel but both the men in her life

were dedicated to them and so she bore up stoically, smearing them with masala, red with Kashmiri chillies, pungent with Goa vinegar. All this to conceal their intense fishiness.

Later, when dinner was done, a call came. It was Jende.

'Can you come?'

'Now?'

'Yes, now. I have that Union here and I need someone else for a change.'

'Unit.'

'That one only.'

'How long has he been there?'

'Five hours.'

Peter sighed. Classic police strategy. Make them talk until they say something.

'Coming.'

Jende was in the back room with Unit, who was in a state close to delirium.

'Motherswear, fatherswear, your swear, I don't know anything.'

Then he saw Peter.

'*Kaka*, you tell them. Kaka, you know me, I know your son. You tell them. I do clean work, respect-wala work. How can I be in kidney selling business?'

Peter noted that the young man had moved him from Chacha to Uncle to Kaka and wondered if there were different degrees of respect and affection hidden in each of them.

'Why would someone call us and give your name, then?' Jende demanded. 'That voice knew a lot about you. He said you kept them in your fridge. Your dead friend was also involved. He was the one who sent kidneys to you regularly to keep for two-three days.'

Peter tried not to look at Jende. Did he really think this was going to work?

But it seemed to have the desired effect.

'Motherswear, sir! No one sent anything to me sir...I swear! And Proxy never sent anything to keep, sir, never—no...yes, there was one thing he sent...'

'See? First they tell lies. Then they say police uses third-degree.' And Jende hit the table: DHUMMM. The effect on Unit was terrible. He burst into the horrible tears of a little boy where sounds are garbled and the breath comes and goes. 'Money,' stood out and 'I didn't want' and 'in the bank'.

Jende heaved himself out of his chair and caused Unit to cower. But the police officer left the room. Peter pulled out a handkerchief and handed it over. Unit grabbed it as if it were a lifejacket thrown to a drowning man.

'Kaka...' he moaned.

Peter leaned in to Unit and put on as ostentatiously considerate a face as he could manage. Hopefully, the boy had not heard of good cop-bad cop.

'Did you kill him?'

'Me?' Sheer outrage made Unit's voice a squeak.

'Then tell the truth, the whole truth. I know the inspector well. Nothing will happen to you if you cooperate with him,' he said. A sex worker, a male prostitute, with a known connection to the dead man—Unit was exactly the kind of person lazy or overworked policemen would pick up to extract a confession and close the case. Unit was lucky Jende was the kind of man who liked to know the truth and would follow it with as much dogged persistence as his calling would allow.

The subject of his thoughts returned and plonked cups of steaming tea in front of everyone. Good cop-good cop, thought Peter.

And so it was that Unit told them his tale, honking into Peter's handkerchief all the while. Pagmat Sir had indeed offered him and Proxy and a third boy called Trophy—Jende raised his eyes skywards—the bathroom facility. There were others too but he could not remember their names.

'Did he touch you?' Jende asked.

'Touch?'

'Did he do any bad things to you?'

'No!' said Unit, completely horrified. 'Sir was not like that.'

Pagmat Senior had seemed to be only interested in improving the quality of India's youth, then, by way of giving them a chance to bathe and to do potty in a clean place. But Pagmat Junior, who stayed for six months with his uncle when he first came to Bombay and joined the police, had proved to be the kind who bullied anything younger and smaller than him. Over ten years older than the boys, he had used his size to harass them. One of his favourite games was to burst in on them and whip off their bathing towels.

So that was how Pagmat Junior had discovered that Proxy was well endowed.

'When we were doing personal training in Prabhadevi, this Pagmat came one day and asked Proxy to meet him,' Unit was saying. 'I told him, don't go, he's not a good person. But he told Proxy it was nothing, he would make Proxy rich, this that.'

Jende nodded.

'He said, all you have to do is stand. Means when someone touches, that's when he would come and take both in. That was all, he said, simple.'

'Honey trap,' said Jende.

'I am also ekyupped.' Unit seemed unable to resist adding this bit of information. 'But I was too blacky so who would come?'

'When did all this happen?'

'Two, maybe three years ago.'

'How much did he earn?'

'He said the cops take seventy, he gets twenty.'

'And who gets the other ten per cent? The man above?'

'No, sir, there is the police station officer in-charge. He also has to get.'

Jende shook his head. The secret of efficient corruption was to feed everyone. Those left unfed were the ones who squealed.

Unit continued: 'Haan. Then one day, he came home and he said, Keep this box.'

'He?'

'Proxy. He came with money in the box. I said: please put it in the bank and he said: you are my bank. I said: this is a big risk, but he gave me friendship *ka vaasta*. He said, you won't do this much for me, who else do I have? So I kept it.'

'Where is this money?'

'I gave it to my mother to keep,' said Unit. 'I think she gave it to my Aaji.'

'So she has the money?'

'No. Just before that night, Proxy came to my home. He said he wanted the money. He said he had committed a crime. He said he had hurt someone, that someone had died and he wanted to give the money back. I said: saying sorry doesn't bring a dead man to life, now let it be, don't get involved any more. But he said: I have to give it back, I feel bad. Then the next day, he was dead.'

Proxy wanted to return some money? To whom?

'Why did he give you the money?'

'Because I was always keeping his money for him and for Trophy. Otherwise they would just spend and spend. They were like that, they had no control.'

'What happened to Trophy?' Peter had to ask.

'Kaka, he has gone to the Gulf. He keeps telling me to come there.'

'Why didn't you go?'

'Where is the money? You need money. For the agent. For the job. For the flight. I didn't have. My mother said: take my gold, but I couldn't. Now I think I made a mistake.'

'That money?' Jende said. 'Whatever he gave you? Maybe you could have gone with that.'

Unit looked uncertainly at him. Jende's face remained unmoving, like a slab of volcanic rock.

Unit looked him in the eye now. 'He trusted me, sir. It was not my money.'

Ten

The next morning, it was a phone call from Jende that woke Peter up.

'Get ready. I will be there in ten minutes.'

'Twenty,' said Peter.

'Ten, Pittr, this is important.'

Fifteen minutes later, he ran down the steps to find Jende parked near the bus-stop.

'Where are we going?' he asked as he got on to the back of Jende's motorbike. This was his least favourite way of being transported around the city. There was no comforting metal cocoon around him and everywhere, monstrous trucks and homicidal cars seemed intent on knocking the motorcycle over. And he always ended up with an ache, somewhere south of the border.

'Durra's place,' said Jende.

'The cop? Your special appearance fellow?'

'Haan.'

'What's he done now?'

'Nothing. His son is dead.'

'*Dead*? How?'

'That we will find out there. Zurale called me, said I should come.'

Jende shot through traffic lights and scattered pedestrians like leaves before the wind. They rode down the highway, Peter holding his breath and Jende snarling at everyone and everything.

Durra lived in a two-bedroom house in Andheri East in a new cooperative housing society. The door of the flat hung open, a sure sign that death had visited. Inside several men were standing around awkwardly, saying nothing, looking at each other and shaking their heads from time to time. But when Peter and Jende came in, they all looked in one direction, as if to point, without recourse to the embarrassment of words, at the corner where a woman sat with a child in her lap.

Peter had never found it easy to enter a house of mourning but one in which a child lay dead was particularly hard. The very size of the body seemed a reproach. 'Could you not have prevented this?' the frail limbs seemed to ask. 'Was it not your turn before mine?' The little body in its Angry Birds T-shirt and shorts—he could not look at it, he could not look away. As a compromise, he looked at the woman who was holding it.

She was weeping with her eyes closed, her arms a tight vise around the corpse of her child. When Jende gestured, one of the men in the room made an attempt to take the child away but was fended off with such ferocity that he fell back. The limbs of the child moved oddly with the motions of the mother's body, jerked about like a marionette, an ugly pretence of life. Jende tried to get her to release the body and was given the same treatment.

Jende asked where Durra was. One of the men waved to the door of the bedroom. Durra was sitting on the bed, listless, staring at the floor. He was not alone but he could well have been. The men who were in the room were looking at him but they could not breach the stronghold of his grief. They had no words to say and no way to say them. Jende looked at him and suddenly turned into a senior officer.

'DURRA,' he snapped the word out, biting down hard on the last consonant. The sheer harshness of his voice made all the men jump. Durra looked up.

'What happened?'

Durra's face went through a bizarre series of contortions. Peter thought that if someone were to film it and slow it down, he might be able to decipher some of the emotions, but he wasn't sure. Grief and rage and guilt and shame and...

Then Durra got up and ran out of his own home, as if the devil were pursuing him. This was so sudden no one even thought to stop him. Jende turned to the assembled gathering.

'Who called me?'

Zurale, the young police officer, detached himself: 'I did, sir.'

'So why did you call me?'

'I think this might also be a police case, sir.'

'Means?'

'I think the boy was murdered, sir.'

'Why?'

'Remember the number written in the station toilet?'

'Yes?'

'There is two written outside the house.'

They went back out again. Indeed the numeral 2 was written outside the house, in red paint.

'What is this?' Jende asked of one of the neighbours.

The man shrugged and made to leave.

'What is this flat number?'

'Durra sahib is flat four.'

'Is there a doctor in the building?'

Just then a new voice cut in.

'What happened here? What's all this?'

It was a young woman, in a white sari with a blue border.

'Arre, their baba is dead,' said the neighbour.

'Dead? What happened? Accident?'

'You are?' Jende asked.

'Nurse,' the woman replied. She was there, she said, to give the child an insulin shot. He had infantile diabetes.

'Arre,' said the neighbour, garrulous with the energy of dammed words suddenly released, 'someone already came and gave the child a shot. Ten minutes later we heard bhabhi shouting. When we ran here it was all over, he had gone.'

'Who came?' the nurse asked.

'I don't know who, but the boy was fully fine yesterday. Playing, jumping, everything,' said the neighbour.

'Something wrong with the injection. Maybe it was *nakli*,' said another man.

'Or there was air bubble. I read that an air bubble in an injection can kill you.'

The nurse was already inserting her way past everyone, easing her professional self into the situation. When she went in and said 'Bhabhi' in a gentle voice, the first response came.

'Arre Rosamma Sister, you have come? You have come? Here is my baba. Please make him all right. Please give him back to me. Please bring him back to me. You are a nurse. You are a devi. You know how much I loved my child. Bring him back to me.'

The men twitched and moved from foot to foot, discomfited.

'Show me,' said Sister Rosamma and perhaps it was the tone of her voice, the suggestion that a nurse might find a way to breathe life into the child, but the child was finally out of the arms of his mother and the investigation could proceed.

After the nurse had checked the child thoroughly, sighing and clucking, Jende picked up the limp body gently, tenderly, and turned around. No one seemed willing to take it so he began to walk slowly out of the house.

'Where are they taking my child, where are they taking my Munna?' the mother began to wail and now things settled into the normal routine. The other women began to swarm into the house to surround the bereaved woman and to give her support and succour.

Rosamma came up to the policemen at the door and said, 'Wait, one minute.'

She popped into the kitchen and opened the fridge. Her face turned grave. She looked at a schedule held to the front of the fridge with a magnet.

'There should be six bottles here,' she said. 'None are left.'

She turned to Jende.

'Whoever gave Munna his shot wanted to kill him. He gave him an insulin overdose.'

A cold hand touched the back of Peter's neck. Jende said nothing. He looked down at the small face, still and silent. He shook his head. Rosamma's eyes were wet but she suddenly wiped them with the back of her hand and drew her small form together.

'May I go, Inspector?' she asked. 'I have four other patients who need their shots.'

'I will let you go as soon as I can. Were you supposed to come today?'

Sister Rosamma shifted a bit.

'I come once a week to check his sugar levels and to see him,' she said. 'I tried to teach them how to give him his shots but they could not. They did not want to learn. So there are these paramedics who come and give the shots.'

But when pressed, Sister Rosamma confessed that she did not have a fixed day for this check-up. She came because of an old favour Durra had done her—a family flat in Malad rented out, a tenant who would not vacate. She tried to make her visits once a week but sometimes...

A neighbour came in to say that Mrs Durra was asking for Sister.

'Call the *gaadi*,' Jende said to Zurale, cop code for the mortuary van.

'I have called, sir,' said Zurale. Now there was nothing to do but wait.

The kitchen seemed small now although it was a medium-sized room. There was nowhere to set down the body, no place that seemed right. The neighbours watched from a distance. Jende stood with the child in his arms, a figure carved in stone.

'What kind of a madman?' Peter asked, aware that he too was using a cliché.

'Sir?'

It was Zurale.

'I am thinking, it was someone who wanted us to know that this is a murder case.'

'Means?'

'The child was diabetic. This could have been a mistake.'

'No one makes a mistake like that, ahn,' said Sister Rosamma pugnaciously. 'In the post mortem, you could tell. This much insulin in the body—it cannot be a mistake.'

'You think they would want a post mortem?' Zurale asked.

Peter thought: he's right. Families did not like taking their dead for post mortems. As though echoing his thoughts, Zurale said: 'They don't like to do that. They would have thought, he had diabetes, he was ill, he died. And even if there was a post mortem, the insulin would have to be there, na? It was not a poison, something that should not be in the child's body.'

'We might not have known,' said Jende. 'Except for that number on the wall.'

Zurale was right. The murderer had wanted them to know.

'Check the dustbin,' said Jende. Zurale rooted about under the kitchen counter and came up with a dustbin. He looked at Jende who jerked his chin at him.

'Go on,' he said. 'You can't be a Brahmin in the police force.'

Peter found some old newspaper and spread it on the floor.

'What am I looking for?' Zurale asked, hitching his trousers up as he prepared to kneel on the floor.

'I don't know,' said Jende.

Zurale looked down at the mess in front of him: chicken bones, fruit peels, balled-up paper, hair balls, pencil shavings.

'What should you be looking for?' Jende asked.

Zurale thought about it for a bit.

'Something he might have left behind?'

'Haan!' said Jende triumphantly. 'Like?'

'Gloves? Insulin bottles? A syringe?'

Jende nodded approvingly and Zurale glowed before snapping gloves on to his hands and setting to work. But for all that there was nothing, just the detritus of the day. The mortuary van came and Mrs Durra screamed and wept and tried to tear her hair and Sister Rosamma gave her a sedative and they left, ashamed of how much relief they felt.

~

They drove back to Mahim on Jende's motorcycle; to the familiar sanctuary of Jende's corner: the table at the far end of the room, the barred window, the neat mess of registers and papers, the paperweight with a single blue fish frozen in its glass enclosure.

But when they arrived, they knew something had blown through the police station, something like a cyclone, even though there was nothing out of place, no chair overturned, no doors ripped off their hinges.

It was the quiet, a chilly quiet. As if everyone were waiting in suspended animation.

'What?' Jende demanded.

'He's waiting for you,' said a junior officer and pointed.

At Jende's desk sat Durra, his hands folded in his lap. A revolver was lying on Jende's table, in front of him.

'What's all this, Durra?' Jende asked, his voice reassuring and gruff, man to man. It said: Yes, I know you've been through a rough patch but you'll pull through.

But even as Jende was sitting down, he used an old newspaper to pick up the revolver and dump it in his drawer and slam it shut and lock it, while managing to suggest that this was merely a piece of everyday business.

'I killed him,' said Durra with no expression in his voice. 'Now it is finished.'

'Who did you kill?'

'Pagmat. I killed him.'

There was a moment's silence.

'Zurale, call a magistrate,' said Jende.

'Sir?'

'If he's making a confession, let him make it in front of a magistrate. I don't want any problems later.'

Zurale went off and Jende said to the man who was his colleague and was now a criminal, 'You want tea?'

'I want my son back. I only want my son back.'

There was silence.

The magistrate came and took his place. A stenographer had come with him, a middle-aged man with pronounced body odour. Zurale also set up his smart phone to take down Durra's confession. There were very few questions. Durra wanted to talk. He wanted to tell them about how his buddy, Pagmat, had suggested the whole honey trap scheme, how he even knew where they could find the boys who would be their bait.

'It was his idea,' said Durra. 'He said it would be a good way to earn money. We didn't have to do anything. We just had to wait. That boy would go into the toilet. He would take it out and make it stand. Then he would wait. He would not let any poor person touch him. When someone from a good family came forward and showed interest, then we would move in. We would take them both away to the police station on the platform at Dadar, we had an arrangement there. Then one of us would take the boy into the next room and pretend to whip him. We would hit a table and the boy would shout and scream. Then we would tell the man to go and bring money.'

Peter suddenly wondered if Leslie had ever had this happen to him. He had described it so accurately.

'How much money?'

'At first, we would say two-three thousand but we saw they were ready to give that much without complaint. So we made it five thousand. If they said maybe and please and cried too much, we would take less because we didn't want to waste time. But never less than two or three thousand each time. We made sure the parties were people who could afford that much. Pagmat said they would spend that much on taking their families to a multiplex in one evening and not think about it.'

'But what if the man said he didn't have the money on him?'

'They all have cards now, credit cards, debit cards. If they had come without their wallets, only carried some notes, we would say, you go and get it. We would keep the mobile phone with us so they would come back. They would lock their phones. One of them didn't. He was so frightened, he forgot and he ran. That was when Pagmat got the idea. He called himself from the man's phone and got his number. Then we took down all his numbers so we wouldn't have to bother with going out in the night. We could just get the money when we wanted. We know who you are, Pagmat told him when he came back. We have your number, we have the numbers of your office, your family, we'll find out all their addresses. Then Pagmat took the man's photo on his phone. See this, he said, we can come to your office, your house and arrest you for gandugiri. Now you arrange good money or you are finished. The man began to cry like a child.'

'Who was this?'

'I don't remember his name.'

'What do you mean…?' Jende began.

Peter sent him a warning look and made a calming motion with his hand. Jende reined himself in with a great and deliberately visible effort and gestured to Durra to continue.

'Do you have his number?'

'Haan,' Durra said and took out his phone and scrolled up and down. Then his face fell. 'I saved his number under X.'

'X?'

'It was Pagmat who made the calls. And who gives his real name in that kind of business? We didn't need to know his name. Pagmat had warned him—we'll know if you change your number, we have all your contacts, we have your address. We didn't, but he believed us.'

'How much did you take from him?'

'When he came back with five thousand, I think, we said, tomorrow morning bring ten thousand and take your phone. He said he had some problems and he needed the money for something or the other, I don't know, debts or down payment or maybe illness in the family, I forget now. But Pagmat said that they would all say the same thing. Pagmat said he was lying. And I listened to him. I should not have listened to him. We asked for another ten thousand, then twenty-five. He should not have given that much, that was his mistake. Once he did, we knew that he had much more and he would give, that he was so afraid he would give us everything till he had nothing to give. I even thought, why doesn't he fight us, tell us to go do what we want? But he only cried and gave and gave. I have not seen a man so afraid. That spoiled Pagmat.'

'Meaning?'

'He enjoyed humiliating the man. Sometimes, he made

this man come to his home. I told him: don't let him come home. He should not know anything about us. But he said: Let him do the work. Then he called him to this station once. Late night, at the back, behind that wall. He made the man kneel before him. I walked away from there. I stopped going with him for the money after that. Only once I went after that, and the man was crying so much I thought there must really be trouble. But Pagmat said it was just acting, when you lose money, you can cry because your heart is breaking, nothing more. I would not have taken all his money. But Pagmat kept saying, he works in a foreign bank, he can get money, let him take a loan, let him do whatever he wants, why does he do these things, if he didn't do randigiri then he wouldn't be in trouble. So I let it continue. But I told them, enough from this man, there are others. But they weren't listening. They took more and more money. Pagmat went and sometimes Proxy.

'You didn't go?'

'I went alone only once. But I gave him some money back because he was saying he didn't have anything, so Pagmat got angry and said I shouldn't go because we must not be soft. But then he killed himself, that fellow. And Proxy said he wanted to stop doing this. He would not go into that toilet again. We told him that he was no one to tell us when he was going to stop. We would tell him when he should stop.'

Durra looked up now, as if emerging from a dream. Jende met his gaze.

'All this was his idea. All this. I told him when I got the first note...'

'What note?'

'It came on a postcard. You will die, it said.'

'Postmark?'

'No postmark. It was hand-delivered here. No one knew when I asked.'

'Fingerprints?'

'I tried at home with talcum powder but there was nothing.'

'Where is it now?'

'I tore it up.'

Jende sighed heavily.

'First, I thought it was just someone trying to frighten me. We are police. Who will try to kill us?'

'You thought about that when you decided to become a blackmailer?'

The magistrate coughed.

Jende forced a smile.

'Sorry,' he said to Durra. Durra tried to smile but his face was trapped in stone. A rictus appeared and vanished.

'I told him. Let's stop. We had done it for three-four years. He had bought a flat. I had cleared my loan. That boy had enough money to go to Dubai. Now one man alone had given us more than we made in six-seven months, and then he had taken his life. I said, let's not do this anymore. He kept saying: one more time, one more time. I want to do this, I want to go to Bangkok. You also come. It was a *nasha*. We should have stopped. If we had stopped then my son would be alive.'

He stopped and looked around at all of them. It seemed as if an animal cunning entered his eyes.

'That man who killed himself? He's the one. His *bhoot* has come back to haunt us. His bhoot killed Proxy. His bhoot came to kill my son. And then I knew what he wanted. He wanted me to kill Pagmat.'

He stopped and then his eyes lost focus. He seemed to be on the verge of hysteria.

'Are you happy now?' Durra was no longer speaking to them. He was speaking to the ghost who walked through his dreams. 'I have killed him. You have taken my son. It is over. Please go now. Please leave me alone.'

Had he thought this through? Peter wondered. Was he going to pretend that he was mad? Claim that as a defence?

And then Durra took out another revolver, put it into his mouth and shot himself.

Eleven

Later, all Peter could think was: so much blood. Who would have thought the man would have so much blood in him?

The apparat of the state took over after that, not very efficient but everyone with a role. A constable found a sheet to cover the body. It was not very clean; perhaps it had done such service before. Zurale was told to inform the deceased's wife. The young officer seemed to be in a state of shock, shaking his head from time to time as if to dispel something hanging around him.

A senior officer visited, took off his cap and stood silently by the body. Everyone else in the room stopped what they were doing and stood up too. A constable asked if the senior officer would like to see. He shook his head, frowned slightly and went into a huddle with Jende. Peter was asked if he would be a witness and agreed. Then a cascade of paperwork began and they signed everything, here and there and once again on the side, initials only. Peter noticed a faint tremor in Jende's hands.

When they were done, he went home and took Jende with him. Millie took one look at them and said that she was going to see her sister in Bandra. Sunil was nowhere about.

'What happened?' she asked at the door, sotto voce.

'A policeman killed himself,' he said. She crossed herself and began to whisper the prayer for the dead. He joined her and felt a finger of warmth uncoil somewhere. How did she know the right thing to do? He kissed her on the top of her head in gratitude and she smiled slightly and left.

In the veranda, Jende had the chair leaning back and his feet up on the railing. Peter opened the bottle of RC and wondered if it would be enough. He poured a Patiala for himself and one for Jende.

'Case closed?' he said.

'Haan, if you believe in *bhoot-pret*,' said Jende. 'That man's ghost killed everyone. But this is not a Ramsay Brothers film.'

Jende swigged. Then he wiped his mouth with the back of his hand, deliberately workmanlike.

'Let's go back, step by step. This case begins with a body in the toilet. This is that fellow they call Proxy. He is working with two policemen. They send him in and lure people out and blackmail them. Then they hit the jackpot. They find someone who has money, big money, and he keeps giving it to them.'

'He must be terrified of something.'

'Why are you saying it as if it is some mystery? He worked in a bank, Durra said. If a man works in a private bank, he's probably on a contract. No union to protect him, but even if there is, the union may not bother about a chhakka. So if they find out, he loses his job. Not only that, he loses face in society. Maybe he loses his friends if they feel others will think they are also like that. He loses his wife and kids if he's married, or loses their respect. Or of his parents, brothers, sisters. He loses his dignity. A man like that has a lot to lose, Pittr.'

Just then Jende's phone rang.

'Zurale?'

He listened for a while and then said: 'Send me an SMS.' Then he looked at Peter.

'They have found out the name of Mr X in Bombay.'

Peter raised his eyebrows in a silent question.

'Sooraj Patel.'

Peter shot up in his chair.

'The man who killed himself. Remember? The piece of paper we found in that Proxy's room?'

'Remind me.'

With growing excitement, Peter filled him in.

'This must have been the man to whom Proxy wanted to return the money. Because Sooraj Patel's mother-in-law did have a medical problem, she was in hospital. There's one way to find out. I've kept that cutting. Lucky I didn't listen to you and put it in the raddi!'

He went off and looked for the paper cutting.

'Here it is: the Badama Hospital. That's where she died.'

Jende looked at his watch.

'Too late to go now. We will see in the morning.'

His phone beeped. A text message. He read it and his face went expressionless.

'Now I also have to go through an inquiry.'

'What inquiry?'

'Arre, that magistrate has gone back and said—Why did I not check Durra for a gun?'

'He put his gun on the table. I saw you lock it in your drawer. Who would have thought he'd have another one?'

'It was Pagmat's gun, not his own,' said Jende. 'Actually, he fooled me very well, putting that gun on the table.'

'Gosh,' Peter said after a moment. 'He planned his suicide? And a policeman killing himself—you don't expect that.'

'More common than you think. This city holds the record. Sometimes nearly 200 kill themselves in a year.'

Peter was silent. That invincible policeman of Everyman's nightmares was sick himself, eaten away from within. He had seen the reports, of course, but no one, as far as he could see, had ever asked why policemen were killing themselves. When a reporter did bother to ask that question, the answers rarely seemed substantial. Yes, they were under serious stress. Yes, they saw the worst society had to offer. But what was it that made some of them take the final decision? Was the worm i' the bud in the first place? Was it because they had expected that the uniform and the stick would give them some way to handle a world that did not make sense?

'I can appear as a witness for you,' he said, finally.

Jende shook his head pityingly. 'It is not that kind of inquiry.'

In his voice, a door closed. Peter was outside, looking in at a khaki world, run by its own laws. There was no room for him in there.

Jende was speaking again: 'So out of all this we know who killed Pagmat and Durra: Durra. But we don't know who killed Proxy and we don't know who killed the child.'

'We also know that this killer wants someone to know that he's taking these lives,' Peter reminded him. 'Did Pagmat get any postcards?'

'Means?'

'Durra got a postcard, right? Warning him? Did Pagmat?'

'Pagmat? How could the killer know that Durra was going to kill....No, you're saying that this is just like a bit of luck for the killer. He wanted to take Pagmat next. Only Durra did the job for him. But he must have warned Pagmat too.'

'Only one thing to do.'

Jende got up and stretched. 'We have two visits to make tomorrow.'

He swigged the whisky remaining in his glass and said: 'Or you may have to go if they decide to suspend me.'

~

No word came of any suspension and so Jende and Peter found themselves at the Badama Hospital. This turned out to be a private nursing home that took up two floors in a five-storey building.

'Who is in charge?' Jende asked the receptionist, a young woman with a vividly painted face. She pointed silently at a door that said Mr A.B. Badama, who turned out to be a nondescript man with a wispy moustache.

'You are the doctor in charge?' Jende asked.

'Oh no, I am not a doctor,' said Badama. 'I am the manager.'

'Who's the doctor in charge?'

'Of which patient?'

'Mrs Hemalata Jugalkishore Patel.'

'Is she with us?' Badama asked but this was a matter of form more than anything else. Recognition had already dawned.

'No, she died here.'

Badama folded his arms and sat back in his chair. 'Oh no, this sad event did not happen here. She was taken home and she expired.'

'I would like to see her records,' said Jende.

'I am not sure...'

'This is a murder investigation, Mr Badama. I can come back with lots of policemen and make lots of noise.'

The arms were unfolded and the manager sat upright in his chair. 'She was an old lady with a kidney problem, sir. She was in bad health but her son would not recognize it. He kept saying, we will find a donor, we will find a donor. Now this is not allowed, of course, but he said it was a member of the family and he arranged for the doctor from Sri Lanka to come. But till the day of the operation there was nothing, no money, no deposit, so we had to cancel the whole thing.'

'I would like to see the file, please.'

The file was handed over

'You will please return when done with it?'

Jende nodded and wrote out a rough receipt.

Outside, he said, 'And now to Pagmat's.'

~

The woman who came to the door was in a white sari but in no other way did she look like she was in mourning for her husband. Her eyes were cold and clear. When Jende introduced himself she led them into the sitting room and instructed an older woman, a family member of some sort, to make tea.

'What do you want?' she asked, settling into the sofa

'I want to know if your husband was bothered about anything in the last few days.'

'Why?'

Peter had never seen Jende as flustered as he was by this simple question.

'We have a murder to clear up here.'

'What murder? My husband's? I know who did it. You know who did it. And we both know that he has got his punishment.'

Peter saw his friend struggle to hold her steel gaze.

'That L.S. Parthusta.'

'And what has my husband to do with that?'

'Your number was found...'

'He was my personal trainer, yes.' She said this with no inflection at all.

'We are still not sure...'

'Inspector Jende, my husband gave his life for the police. He is dead. He was killed by another policeman. Now what is left to say? Why have you come here?'

The older woman brought two cups of tea and put them down with distinct unfriendly clicks. They sat there sipping their tea.

Jende tried again: 'If your husband gave his life for the police, he would want Proxy's case cleared up too.'

'Proxy?'

'Your personal trainer.'

'It is very sad that he should die. But I don't know how to help you.'

'I would like to look at his things,' said Jende.

'Go ahead,' she said and pointed to a desk in the corner. 'That is where he kept everything.'

The desk was standard office supply, brown Formica top over iron legs painted green. The surface was completely clear, as if everything had been swept off.

'Was there anything here? Did you throw anything away?' Jende asked.

'No. He kept it like that.'

The top drawer was full of bills and receipts; the second was filled with bank material, the third had a postcard right on the top that said: *Ab teri baari*. You're next.

Jende grunted.

'Found what you want?' she asked.

'Thank you. I'm taking this as evidence.'

'Of what?'

'I will let you know,' he said. He wrote out a receipt for her but she did not take it from his hand. Instead, she tilted her chin at the table and he placed it there.

They left without finishing their tea.

~

'These days, see how things have changed,' Jende said as they waited for their filter coffee in an Udipi restaurant. 'People have started threatening the police. When I joined the police, I didn't think anyone would have the guts.'

'Did you think policemen would go around finding young men to stand in toilets to blackmail gay men?'

Jende shot him a look but just then the coffee came and so he contented himself with stirring it vigorously and frowning at it.

'I think, Pittr, you were right,' he said. 'We have to look at this Sooraj Patel again.'

Peter nodded. It was as much of an admission as he would get.

'I will get his file out and see,' said Jende. 'You go and talk to people in his area.'

'I already have,' said Peter guiltily. 'That journalist Jotin Perry...'

'Where did you go?'

'I met the widow.'

'Offo,' said Jende, annoyed. 'Now I will have to go and ask questions.'

'Can we get Sooraj Patel's phone records?'

'What do you think you'll get there?'

'I don't know. I can't think of anything else to do.'

'Do you want to see them? Or Zurale could make a list of people called.'

'That would be good,' said Peter and Jende rose to attend to it.

'Chalo, I will drop you home.'

Twelve

'What do you know about Proxy?' Peter asked Sunil. His son had just finished a long telephone call and was now drinking his second cup of tea.

'What is this about, Dad?' Sunil asked, suspiciously.

'He's dead and I'm helping Jende find out who killed him.'

Sunil looked at him carefully.

'Call it deep background,' said Peter. Sunil relented.

'I don't know much. He would call from time to time. Sometimes he just needed to talk. Sometimes he called because he could. Once or twice, drunk.'

He thought for a while.

'There was another guy who knew him well. A friend of his.'

'Unit?'

'Yes. I've met him a couple of times. I think I even have his number somewhere,' he began to flick through his phone. Peter sighed. Did the boy have every number of every male prostitute in town? Then he saw Sunil raise the phone to his ear.

'Unit? It's me. Sunil bhaiyya.'

There was a pause.

'Yes, I heard. Very sad.'

Another pause.

'My father wanted to meet you.'

A pause and then Sunil laughed politely.

'Come for lunch.'

Peter's blood froze. What was the boy doing?

But it was done, the invitation was accepted and the address was being dictated, along with directions about the bus-stop near Shobha, a famous restaurant that served as their landmark.

'That's done,' he said, when he'd disconnected.

'What's done?' asked Millie, coming out into the veranda with an old aluminium kettle with which she watered the tiny kitchen garden that struggled into green life in a corner.

'Someone's coming to lunch,' said Sunil airily.

'Who is it?'

'His name is Unit.'

There was a moment of silence in the veranda. Millie stopped watering and looked at both of them. Peter was vaguely aware that he looked guilty. 'Who is this Unit?'

'He's a...'

'Sex worker,' interrupted Sunil.

'What?'

'I wanted to talk to him about this murder in which Sunil...' Peter said and the cat was truly out of the bag.

Millie ignored her tulsi, the pride of her garden, from which she was wont to force feed him a couple of leaves when she remembered.

'Peter, this is the ghastly limit. And lunch? Today?'

'Maa, it's only ten. There's time. We don't need a feast. And it's important, no? Dad wants to ask him some questions about his friend who was murdered.'

'My, this gets better and better. We're going to have a sex worker to lunch who has a friend who got murdered. Does he also do some smuggling on the side?'

Both the men in her life recognized this as rhetorical and stayed silent.

'I hope he isn't vegetarian?' she said next and both men

took this as gracious acceptance of a situation beyond her control.

'I know he eats chicken at least,' said Peter and the matter was resolved. He followed her into the kitchen.

'One of you will have to get a broiler from Mafco,' she said.

'I'll go,' said Sunil.

'Put on outside shorts,' said his mother automatically.

'What's wrong with these?' said Sunil even as he wandered off to find something more suitable for public viewing.

Millie poked about for the jar of basmati rice.

'Thank you,' said Peter.

'For what?' Millie asked.

'I don't know. For tolerating us, I suppose. Father and son.'

'This is what I got,' she said and shrugged.

'Maybe he'll adopt.'

'And maybe he won't,' said Millie. 'Maybe Mother Mary wanted grandchildren too.'

That startled a laugh out of him.

~

Unit was punctual, for in Mumbai, if you are fifteen minutes late you are exactly on time. Sunil opened the door to him and was greeted with a great deal of enthusiasm, a firm handshake and a hint of a bow. Millie was gracious, if slightly wary, but when she saw how clearly overawed the boy was by his surroundings, she thawed somewhat. Besides, Unit had clearly dressed for the occasion: he was wearing a white long-sleeved button-down shirt tucked into blue jeans, and sneakers which he took off at the door.

'Have you come far?' she asked him, as she served him water in a stainless steel glass. Much discussion had preceded this. Millie had been taking out four nice tumblers—not cut-glass but glass made to look like it was—when Sunil told her that this might seem offensive.

'Why?' Millie had asked.

'Because outsiders, whose caste is uncertain, are served in glass.'

'We have no copper, let me tell you.'

'Stainless steel will do,' Sunil said.

'Those everyday glasses?'

'Everyday utensils can sometimes be a compliment,' he said and Millie contented herself with washing them twice over so that they shone. Now Unit drank his water and asked for some more, apologizing and explaining that it was very hot outside. Millie smiled and nodded and said lunch would be ready in ten minutes.

Unit had chosen a cushioned chair next to Peter's, and now he leaned a little towards Peter, as if deriving confidence and comfort from the presence of an old familiar.

'You knew Proxy well, didn't you?' Sunil asked.

'Bhaiya, we grew up together.'

'I remember him, it's sad he had to go that way,' Sunil said. 'No one deserves that kind of death.'

'Everyone says: he did that kind of work and that's why he was murdered. They don't understand that he had to do it.'

'Why did he have to do it?' Peter asked because he thought it was expected.

'Uncle, everything is not about *andhi maa-vidhwa behen*. That fellow up there writes the fate of gutter-worms for some people. But even finding a simple job is difficult. That is also bad kismet. What does one do then?'

'You were trained, no? As personal trainers?'

'That was all *chutiya banaane ka dhanda*. Sorry, should not talk like that but it is true. It's a scam and there are many fools like us. They took the money and then they had some days of classes where they talked about this muscle and that muscle and they taught us some exercises and gave us some notes and took our tests and we all passed. Like whatever you wrote, you passed.'

Sunil pressed on.

'But if everyone has the same kind of certificate, these gyms and clubs and things will hire you, right?'

'I went for one interview after another. You can't imagine where all I went, Sunil Bhaiyya. One place, they said everyone wears shorts here. I said I cannot wear shorts. They said: why not, you have good legs. And you will not believe, Uncle, that time my thighs were like that,' he said, turning to Peter and indicating balloon-like thighs. 'But I said I cannot wear shorts and show my legs and I cannot wear sleeveless T-shirts also. They said, what is your problem? I said I am very blacky. They said, come back when you are less blacky. What to say?'

Millie had just come into the room and heard all this.

'But you should not be ashamed of your skin colour,' she said, setting down a plate of fried chicken in front of him. This was standard Millie procedure. Some bits were fried and some bits went into the curry. When they were eating en famille, the fried chicken came with the meal and could be savoured slowly. When there were guests, the fried chicken became a starter.

'I'm not ashamed, Aunty. I just don't like to show my body.'

Millie looked a bit surprised by this but she decided to let it pass.

'Could Proxy have got those jobs?' Peter asked, trying to steer the subject back to the dead boy.

'He also could not find any. Because he didn't know English. You have to know English for the good-good gyms. If you can speak well, then they hire you. But we couldn't speak and they wouldn't hire.'

'What about you? Did you get work anywhere else?'

'Who would take me if they wouldn't take him?'

Sunil looked at his mother and she rose and went into the kitchen, saying, 'I should warm the *khana*, you men carry on.'

'So Proxy trapped men for the cops. Did he also go with men for money?' Sunil asked. Peter had always known his son to be direct, but he was still taken aback by this.

As was Unit. 'Bhaiya, how can one ask things like that? Who will tell? You think I told him what I did?'

'But what do you think?' Sunil persisted.

Unit looked at him as if he were sorting something out in his head. Then he said: 'See, men like you, you'll go to college and you learn many words for this and that. If you do this, then you're this kind of person. If you do that, then you're that kind of person. For us, we only have one term: enjoy. If we enjoy, we do. We don't need names. If we don't enjoy, we'll do if they give money. Once you take money for this, then everything else is easy.'

Millie returned and Unit went silent.

Lunch was served at the small round dining table for four. This again had caused some consternation and argument prior to Unit's arrival. In the general way of things, the food was placed in serving dishes and the guests were expected to help themselves. Sunil was of the opinion that this might be a little odd for those who were used to dining in thalis, where the mother of the house filled and refilled your *katoris*. But at this Millie cavilled.

'There's chicken fried, chicken curry and pulao. Also raita and aloo jeera. That's not enough for katoris and thalis and I don't know what. Anyway, I'll have to borrow them from Harshaben and she might be horrified that we're serving chicken in her veggie things. So he can eat the way we eat and he can drink the way they drink.'

Unit did not seem discomposed by the bare plate and proceeded to fill it with healthy servings of everything.

'Why are you called Unit?' Millie asked.

'I want to go to Dubai,' said Unit suddenly.

'What will you do there?' Peter asked.

'I will do anything, Uncle. Anything. I will wash toilets, even. But I want to earn money. So much I have to do. I have to buy my own house. I have to repair my house in the village. I have to get married.'

There was a moment of complete silence at this. Peter wondered whether his face showed the same astonishment as Millie's. Sunil's face, he noticed, had arranged itself into a mask of utter neutrality. It must be a professional expression, this one, the kind that allowed the other person no purchase at all.

Maybe this was supposed to allow the other person to be himself or herself. But Peter found it slightly chilling.

Millie served pudding which Unit declined at first but was persuaded to have. It was caramel custard and it was nearly demolished when they were done. Unit rose to go.

'Uncle,' he said, 'about Proxy? Have they found out anything at all?'

'They're trying,' said Peter, not sure how Millie would react to talk of a murdered child and numbers written in blood immediately after lunch.

'See? No one really cares when one of us dies,' Unit said.

Peter wanted to ask who comprised the 'us' but he decided to leave well enough alone.

~

In the evening Jende dropped by for tea and *nankhatai* biscuits.

'I went to see that woman, the widow. She said the press is harassing her,' he looked at Peter who tried not to look too ashamed of his little act.

'Find out anything?'

'No. She talked too much, and only about herself. She's from Surat. She came here after she got married. She says she did not want to marry this fellow but he had a good job and the family was not asking for dowry and wanted a simple temple *shaadi*. They were a middle-class family that had fallen on bad times after the father died, she said, so the mother was happy to accept. She felt something was wrong right then, and after marriage he did not touch her. She's thinking of going back to Surat now but she's also thinking of going abroad because they are more broad-minded there.'

'Is everyone going abroad?'

Jende answered Peter's rhetorical question. 'Anyone who can get out of this *manhoos* place, I suppose.'

'You ever thought of it?'

'No *sarkaari* person ever thinks of going,' said Jende. 'Their children may. Young people want everything today, this minute. No laptop, no car and life is a tragedy.'

He seemed to fall into a reverie at the thought.

'What about the kidney operation?' Peter asked.

'She says she knows there had to be an operation but she doesn't know anything about it. She says it had to do with her mother's kidneys and her brother and her husband were managing all that.'

'This whole thing seems illegal to me,' said Peter.

Jende nodded.

'You know, Pittr, I kept thinking—it is strange, she has family, she did not drop out of the sky, no? But it was like no one exists for her, not even the dead mother. Everything is about her. People can be like that?'

'All kinds, Shiva.'

'Chha,' said Jende.

'Anything on the man who came for Durra's boy?' Peter asked.

'The mother's in no state to talk yet. We asked all the

neighbours, nothing. One or two said it was someone in a uniform, like those people wear in hospitals. Shirt-pant with embroidery on the pocket.'

Jende rode off on his motorbike and Peter went for a walk. He walked the streets in a muddle. There seemed to be no leads and there seemed to be huge leads. Three young men had been taken to bathe in their PT teacher's home. He had no untoward interest in them other than ensuring their hygiene but his nephew, a fresh recruit to the police, had noticed that they were well-endowed and when he thought up his honey trap some years later, he had sought them out. One was too dark of skin to attract customers. One went to the Gulf. The third was slashed open in his workplace and left to die. His kidney had been taken out, but for no apparent reason. Then one of the cops' kids was killed with an overdose of insulin. This was presumably to hurt the man where he was most vulnerable. You take one, we'll take four. Pure rage. He tried to put himself in the mind of the killer, someone who was numbering bodies as they fell. He tried to feel that level of anger. What would it be like if someone hurt…? And then his mind would not allow him to finish the sentence. A superstitious dread sent a shiver down his spine. He returned to the crimes at hand.

The father of the child, deranged with grief, kills the originator of the plan. He knows that his son has been taken from him and he kills his best friend and then kills himself. There was a plan to this, a wholeness. This was no random string of crimes. Everything seemed to track back to the cops and their honey trap. And yet, who could it be who wanted to lash out at them? He shook his head. So much was happening that it seemed as if finally the gods themselves would have to descend and rub his nose in the solution.

And then the next morning, Leslie called Peter and told him that he had killed Proxy, could he please come?

Thirteen

Leslie was in a batik silk kaftan of some antiquity. He was also wearing a necklace of red stones around his neck.

'Garnets,' he said when he caught Peter's eyes on them. 'I thought they were appropriate for confession.'

'Why?'

'Oh, I don't know. I suppose it has to do with the colour of congealed blood or something?'

'No, why did you kill them?'

'Oh no reason at all,' said Leslie airily. 'I am dying. Did you know that?'

'I had heard,' said Peter.

'No one has any privacy these days. I thought this would be a good way to sign out. Leave some mark. Right some wrongs. I did write a novel once. Did I give you a copy?'

'Several,' said Peter.

'I fear I have inflicted multiple copies on the world at large,' said Leslie. 'It does cause a bit of grief when I find my book dumped on a pavement stall at Churchgate. So I decided that I would slip a five-hundred-rupee note in between the leaves of some of the books.'

'Why?'

'Like a reward. For opening the book.'

'Most didn't?'

'Most didn't. But then people are like that.'

'You don't like people?'

'Do you? Perhaps you would. You seem like the kind of person who might. I think loving people is the ultimate racist request. If you're not supposed to hate Blacks because they're Black or gays because they're gay, then why should you love the Chinese because they are the Chinese or hetters because they are hetters? And if you're not expected to do that, then why should you be expected to love the whole human race because it is the human race?'

Peter tried to think up a suitable response. Leslie smiled, coolly compassionate.

'It doesn't matter. It probably comes with the territory. Being Christian and all that, you were taught to love your neighbour as you love yourself.'

'You're Christian too.'

'I tried it, my darling, but the neighbour was far too ghastly and his sons were not interested in my kind of love. And I tried the Church too but it would have nothing to do with me so I decided to have nothing to do with it. And the rest was easy enough.'

'You decided to hate people.'

'I wish I could say I decided to. I don't think I decided anything at all. I think hatred was forced on me. What I loved I could not have. What I could not have, I also loved.'

Peter nodded.

'And then love happened. Do you know what it is like to love in your old age? No, you're happy with your wife and your son. There's nothing you want because you got it all. I didn't have anything when I went to this Gay Bombay bash in Thane. At some terrible fast food place. Can you imagine me in Thane eating a greasy burger? I told the organizers, I said, you'll only find me in Thane when they take me to the mental hospital, my darlings. But one evening, there was an air-conditioned car with enough leg room and there was someone who wanted to go so I thought if I can go in style and come in style, why not? So I went and he was there. He was a clerk type. I mean most of that class, they'll come and they'll say "Suck me" and "I'm straight" and "I'm a top". And they don't want to have anything do to with the word gay, never mind joining the movement or sharing what's going on in their lives and heads. So I thought he's here to get someone to give him an orgasm and then he can go home and pretend to joke about it. I thought I'd just ignore him but I found myself talking to him and then I found myself coming back to Bandra on the train because he had a railway pass, can you imagine? He said why didn't I make a pass and I said I was making one and he said "Good, because you can save money and then you can travel really fast in this city"—and all the other clichés they use when they talk about train travel. So it wasn't even his mind, I have to say. It wasn't his body either. I mean it was okay but it was nothing special. Not his *popat* either.'

Peter hoped things weren't going to get any more explicit.

'He was closeted of course. They all are. Everyone is. One freak of nature came here and said to me that I was closeted because I didn't go out and shout it from the rooftops and give interviews in magazines about it. I said, "Well then this is the best appointed closet I have seen and it's been big enough for me for most of my life but it's feeling a little small right now, so could I ask you to leave?" She was so offended, she could barely speak. That's what I find really annoying about the little queens, you know? They can hand it out but they certainly can't take it. You wouldn't know, would you, dear?'

Peter said, 'You were telling me about the man you met in Thane.'

'He was Bosie to my Wilde, he was Hallam to my Arthur, he was Alcibiades to my Socrates. He was a clerk with six inches to his account. And he had an old mother and he had a couple of older sisters and he had oh I don't know—debts in the village or whatever it is that afflicts the men of that class, but he had it all and so he had to get married and he had to get a dowry so that he could then dowrify his sisters and pay off the zamindar and get his land back. I thought he was telling me this because he wanted me to give him money but he never...'

And at this point, Leslie broke down. It was real sorrow, the kind that smashes through the ironic protection of sophistication and brings with it a very real and ugly weeping. He was crying, his face squinched up, his nose running, and he was making broken mumbles that passed as words.

Peter did not know what to do. He saw a box of tissues and went over to get it.

'If you hand me a tissue, I shall hit you with a pansy,' said Leslie, suddenly overcoming his grief. 'I'm sorry. I spent all that time waiting for him to say, give me money, give me this, give me that, but he didn't, he didn't and if he had he might still have been alive because he could have...'

Once again, he burst into tears. Peter sat frozen. It was a little longer this time, but soon enough Leslie had recovered.

'You should be hugging me, but who knows someone might see you hugging a gay man and think you're also a phoolrani from Mahim. You're all so blasted locked up in your own heads. Oh god, oh god, sometimes I think, I don't really mind dying, because at least all this hetero-crisy will be out of my sight. I mean, hell should be full of the lot of us, right? And there will be no need for pretence. There will be all those poor johnnies who slept with other johnnies and were stoned to death. I wonder if the Islamic gay chaps and the Jewish fellers and the Christians will share the same Circle of Hell?'

This might go on all night, Peter feared.

'Oh but that's not what you came about, is it? I was telling you my story. I was perhaps the first or second man he'd ever had sex with. When he told me that, I said, in an act of charity, my god, I don't even believe how wonderfully sweet I was, I told him he should go out and get some more experience. I can't imagine anyone else saying something like that and me so deeply in love that I wanted to own his earlobes, do you know the feeling?'

Peter tried to nod but couldn't.

'And then your boys got their claws into him. Caught him in a toilet. Was it dear old Matunga? Or some other one? He took all the money meant for his sister's marriage and gave it to these disgusting fellows. And then he couldn't face his sister, so he killed himself.'

Then he paused. Peter waited.

'Oh Peter, Peter, I lost everything in one night, my love and my light, and out of the depths, there rose in my soul a great desire for vengeance. I decided that I would roll down upon them and they would suffer for what they did. After all, I am dying. What have I to lose? I decided to use the old ghost-to-ghost hook-up and spread the word. Pretty soon I heard about this Proxy and his cops. First the boy, I thought. Then the cops. But after the first one, oh brother—the blood all over the place! And one of my favourite jeans ruined. I had to dump it in the Mahim Creek. But later of course, when it was over, I couldn't go home all *nanga panga*.'

'You killed a child?'

There was a pause as Leslie regrouped. As if, Peter thought, he was trying to explain it to himself.

'I wanted to hurt him where it would leave the greatest ache. And it worked rather well, didn't it? They killed each other without my having to raise a finger.'

'A child, Leslie?'

Leslie raised defiant eyes: 'I don't know why we make special cases for children. I mean they're just smaller versions of adults, are they not? And this time I did it easy and smooth, didn't I? I just gave him an insulin shot more than he needed and he went to sleep in his mother's arms. Children die worse deaths in this country, you know.'

Peter sighed. 'You'll have to repeat all this, Inspector Jende is on his way. But keep it short.'

'Do I know the Inspector?'

'No, but he's a good man.'

'I have always relied on the kindness of strangers,' said Leslie and got up from the sofa. The bell rang. Peter went to the door and returned with Jende.

'The good inspector,' Leslie bowed theatrically and sat back on the sofa. 'I'll keep it short, Mr Jende.'

And with some help from Peter, he repeated his confession, clinically, without emotion, taking under ten minutes. Jende listened without comment. Then Leslie was done and said, 'You may arrest me now, Inspector. I'm ready.'

'You might want to change,' Peter said gently.

Leslie looked puzzled and then looked down at himself.

'Dear me,' he said and chuckled a little. 'I had completely forgotten. I am not quite ready for my mid-shot, am I, Mr De Mille?'

He went into his bedroom and rustled and squeaked as he changed.

'*Marega saala, jail mein*,' said Jende, but not without sympathy.

'Marega anyway,' said Peter.

'Means philosophy-style? We are all going to die, *zindagi toh bewafa hai*?'

'No. AIDS.'

'*Aai-la*,' said Jende, reverting to youth. And so it was that when Leslie came out of his bedroom, fetching in a pink T-shirt and jeans, he was not handcuffed as he got into the police jeep. He rode in regally, as if rehearsing lines from various plays that he would try on the judge.

Jende kept looking at him suspiciously. Leslie caught his eye and winked. Jende sighed, a deep annoyed sigh. When they got to the police station, he sent Leslie off to be processed and taken to the Arthur Road jail. Then he took Peter aside.

'You ask him why he's telling lies,' he said. 'You get the truth from him.'

'What?'

'See, he's thinking police want to close the case so they will listen to him. This is true. Police generally want to close the case. But that is not how it is with me, you know that. He's lying. You will get the real story out of him.'

Peter looked at him.

'Then why did we arrest him?'

'It is okay for him to think he's fooling me. I don't mind. And maybe the real killer will think it is okay now and he can relax, and he'll make some mistakes. Now you go to Arthur Road and talk to him. Get the truth.'

But Leslie was not to be moved. He was firm in his resolve: he had killed the man and he had ripped out the kidney. And he had killed the child. He claimed to have been in the grip of a great rage. For having his only chance at love taken away from him, he said; for all the sad and lonely days and nights of his miserable life.

'And yet when I came to talk to you, you were...'

'I put on a great show, didn't I?'

Peter said nothing. Was all this part of the mental problems AIDS brought with it? No, there was too much coherence here.

'Where is your boarder?'

Was it his imagination or was there a moment of unease in Leslie's face?

'Himal? I sent him away last night. I didn't want him mixed up in all this.'

Peter looked carefully at him. Leslie in the garb of a prisoner was a strange thing, almost as if he were naked without his finery. He shook his head. Leslie seemed almost offended at this.

'My dear, you have no idea what a quiet man can do when he is in a rage.'

'In all the years I have known you,' said Peter with some asperity, 'I have never thought of you as a quiet man.'

Leslie actually managed a thin chuckle.

'Oh if you don't make noise, they pretend you don't exist, they pretend your sexuality doesn't exist, they pretend even if they've had you suck their cocks the night before.'

Peter rolled his eyes and went back to the Mahim Police Station.

'No luck,' he said to Jende.

'Case closed,' said Jende. 'And the real murderer is out there.'

They sat in silence.

'He's protecting someone,' said Jende. 'I have seen cases like this where someone is ill and they think, chalo, I will say I did it and this person who has his life in front of him can go and live and I will die.'

'You think?'

'I think. You know why? He's not the kind to cut someone. To cut someone like that is not easy. You need a heart of stone. You have to be able to have blood come *jisshhh-jisshhh* all over you. This kind of fellow? He's then going to put his hand inside and take out a kidney? Oh yes, that he's going to do. And crows will be white and the sun will rise from the west tomorrow.'

All the way home, Peter wondered about this. Could Leslie be protecting someone? It might be. He could have talked himself into a place where he had persuaded himself he was someone in *The Tale of Two Cities*, ready to sacrifice his life for the better man. But who could this better man be whom he was protecting?

Nothing added up.

There was someone else behind him, someone in the shadows.

Fourteen

Unit called later that evening.

'On TV they are saying someone has been arrested?'

'Yes,' said Peter.

'Who?'

'I don't know if you know him. He's a man called Leslie Siqueira.'

'Who?'

'From Bandra.'

'Achcha? He killed Proxy?'

'He says so.'

'Oh *confession*,' said Unit dismissively, 'What's the use of that? They go to court and say that it was because police gave third degree.'

'I don't think this guy will do it.'

'Will he get *phaansi*?'

'I think it's early days to talk about the death penalty,' said Peter cautiously.

'He should get it. He has killed a child.'

'That's for the courts to decide,' said Peter.

'I'm applying for Dubai visa, uncle,' said Unit. 'I'm going for tourist visa to see the place and then decide.'

'Good luck,' Peter said and hung up.

If even Unit was dismissing the confession, merely for being a confession, what hope did Leslie have of being taken seriously? He would be a sensational serial killer if life was a Hollywood film, but Leslie in that toilet?

And yet. Stranger things...And the numbers on the walls, at least one of them written in blood—wasn't that straight out of a film?

No, Peter told himself. Sometimes fiction is stranger than truth. It couldn't be Leslie Siqueira.

Back to square one. If not Leslie, who? What kind of person?

Perhaps it was time to go back to Dr Ajit Pitale.

~

As he dialled the number for Pitale, he remembered the last moment in that office, the question with which he had poured shame over himself. Without wanting to, he set the phone down.

But then he reasoned with himself: 'He will not remember you. He sees a hundred people a day. They pass before his eyes in a parade. It's as if someone who has been interviewed by a reporter once expects to be remembered. Professionals do not remember.'

He made the call and fixed an appointment.

Pitale did not look surprised to see Peter. Perhaps it was part of his stock-in-trade; he was not to show emotion.

'This is about the case I was helping with, the murder in Matunga Road station?' Peter began.

'I assumed that,' said Pitale.

'Well, I feel in some ways this is all tied up with acts—various acts of prostitution,' said Peter, aware that he was fumbling.

'Sex work,' said Pitale.

'Sex work,' said Peter. 'Only, it's not just work, is it? I mean, there's exploitation and lack of consent and...'

'There's a lot of that in this hospital too. In any institution,' Pitale said.

'Yes, but it's not the same, is it?'

'How?'

Peter found himself growing exasperated.

'When I was a young man, I thought—I mean I fantasized about selling my body. I don't know why but I used to think it might be fun to have someone pay me for sex. It seemed so extraordinary that someone would want me...' he tailed off, appalled at what he had told a stranger. However the admission seemed to have caused Pitale to melt a little.

'It's a common male fantasy,' he said. 'Men are used to doing the desiring; they want to be desired. To an adolescent or a young male, the idea that someone is willing to pay means that they are serious about their desire.'

'So they'd be really happy about actually *being* paid, when anybody else would have to pay?'

Pitale raised an eyebrow satirically to signal that he recognized that Peter was playing the straight guy, that he wanted the doctor to know that his fantasies were about women.

'Women may have domination fantasies,' Pitale said, 'and they may like to play them out as long as they feel there is some way in which they can stop when things are getting too much. And that is what fantasies allow us to do: to play out a scene without the problems of reality.'

'I was talking about men, actually. The men who...men in sex work, I mean.'

'Ah,' Pitale suppressed a smile. 'We'll have to first understand that there are very few women clients for it to be a viable profession for the men. So it is MSM sex, mainly.'

'Yes,' Peter said, relieved that he didn't have to ask Pitale to spell out MSM. 'Men who have sex with men,' Sunil had told him. And as he remembered that conversation now, he was surprised that it wasn't worry or confusion that he felt. It was a kind of wonder, mixed with some pride, that he was a father whose son could talk to him about MSM as he might about aerodynamics or the *Communist Manifesto*.

'Now you can't quote me on this,' Pitale was saying. 'I haven't seen any studies. I have no idea if there are some. I don't know how they were conducted.'

'I get that,' said Peter.

'Without going into too many details, the ones I have treated here...'

'You've treated some?'

'Generally, they come in with substance abuse issues. The medical system is so old, and so unprepared, that we take them all into the psychiatric ward: the failed suicides, the anorexic girls, the boys with drug problems...all in one ward.'

Peter was silent.

'But one day things will change,' Pitale smiled, without humour. 'We can't give up hoping.'

The silence grew. Peter tried to be patient and failed.

'The male sex workers?'

'I'm just thinking aloud. How do you connect with your body? How much is you? How much is not? When you put it out on the market, and it is analyzed and assessed and an offer is made, how can that offer not demean you? One of the young men told me that he was saving his seal...'

'Seal?'

'It's a way to talk about virginity. In the brothels, you'll be assured the new intake is "seal-pack". In his case, I suppose he meant anal virginity.'

Peter nodded.

'He said he was saving his seal for a flat. He would only give it to someone who bought him a flat.'

Peter raised his eyebrows.

'Yes. It did seem like a lot of money to be asking but again, this is fantasy surfacing in the middle of reality. He had anal fissures and was HIV positive but he was the young man who was saving his seal for the big sethia who would fall in love with him and keep him in style.'

'It seems that fantasy...' Peter had no way to complete his sentence.

'Fantasy is useful. Fantasy is vital. It keeps sex alive in most marriages. You go to a sex therapist and they'll always tell you about using fantasy. But that's when you're in control of what's happening. When a young man takes that decision, to sell his body, he soon discovers how much is wrong with it. How he can be brutalized by clients. How he can be robbed by the police. He realizes he must always walk that difficult line between advertising his wares and advertising what his work is. He may be the object of desire and make heads turn on the road, even in five-star hotel lobbies; he may seem unattainable to most of the world, but as soon as money enters the equation, this changes. Now he's the whore. He has to do what he is told for his money, he is often abused. His ego is hurt but he does what he is told. He collects his money and his anger builds.'

Anger, Peter thought. It's an epidemic. We're all angry now.

'I have to keep reminding you that I'm not an expert. I've talked to seven or eight men in sex work. They all began voluntarily. Someone told them they were good-looking, women would pay, it would be easy money. And then they found that it was the men who would pay. Now they're in difficult territory already because they're in direct competition with hijras. The hijras were traditionally the ones who serviced men who wanted anal sex. I don't think it's that simple, though, I don't think men who sleep with hijras are necessarily gay; I think it's much more complex and tells you something about how fluid sexuality is. You may want a hijra, specifically. Or you may even love someone who just happens to be a hijra. It's never easy but when you're a young man who's selling his body to other men, you're now like a hijra. And I have yet to meet a man who thinks being called a hijra is not an insult.'

'Surely some of them are gay?'

Pitale shrugged.

'I think those are tags, labels. They're not particularly useful. Yes, some of them may be homosexual but this anger isn't about orientation. In sex work, it's not about your orientation. It's about being paid. And here I want to make a bigger case about money, if I may. No one is ever happy with what they are paid. I have heard my fellow doctors complain about their salaries, I've heard CEOs complain about their pay packets. We've made an offering of the self to the world and it has responded with *this*? Now when you're doing that with your body, it's likely to be even more terrible when you feel undervalued, when you're not suddenly treated like a king but a *randi*—you'll be surprised how often that word is used in male sex work.'

'Doesn't anyone leave, find a way out?'

'I'm sure some do. But I think there are many who can't get off because there's always money to be made, there isn't a ceiling—paradoxically, they feel in control; they can go out anytime and at the end of fifteen minutes, an hour, there'll be money. A few thousand, a few hundred. But the longer they're in it, the harder it is to get out and greater the sense of debasement. And sometimes something snaps. It's usually rage, directed at themselves, at the world. It's the same everywhere, isn't it? The corporate boardroom, the bedroom or that railway station toilet—men who think they've lost power are prone to violent rage and it may be a long time before they emerge from it, if they emerge at all.'

~

On his way back from Pitale's, Peter found himself walking to the nearest station and getting on to a train. He found he was on his way to Andheri. Perhaps there was something to be found out there, some last clue.

The three men were under the tree as if they had not moved.

'Hello,' he said.

'Hello,' said one of them.

'You have come before,' said another. 'You are that journalist fellow's friend. I told him to write about how the zopadpatti is robbing electricity but these journalists are all cowards. There was a time when the *Free Press Journal* would stand up to the government also. Now they are all sell-outs.'

Peter sat down.

'Yes, they only write about murder and suicide,' he said.

'You are very interested in suicide,' said the second gent. 'Last time also you were asking about it.'

'That woman is going away now, you know? I am told Rahina Saahab is looking for a boarder again.'

'Where will he get one in this market? Do you know what he's asking for that house?'

Peter intervened.

'Did you know him, the dead man?'

'Sooraj Patel? Haan. I met him in the lift once. I told him. I said, this is a *shareefon ki basti*. We are all decent family people. You have to live properly if you want to live here or you'll be thrown out. I will talk to the society, I said.'

'What was he doing?'

'Every night he came home late. God knows where he was going and what he was doing. As if he had another life, indecent fellow.'

The men began to talk about other people who flouted the laws of the society. Karambelkar who parked in other people's slots when they went out of town. De Souza who fed the street dogs although they howled all night and kept the *shareefon ki basti* from sleeping. Peter got up and was about to leave when he was confronted by Himali herself.

'What are you doing here?' she asked him sharply.

'I was about to...'

'What kind of security is this, Mr Sheorey?' she asked one of the old men trenchantly. 'Anyone can walk in and harass young women.'

'What's going on here?' asked another voice. 'Who is harassing my sister?'

Behind her stood Himal.

Himal and Himali.

So this was why the young man had looked familiar that morning in Bandra.

Himali Patel must once have been Himali Shah. She had changed her name. Most women still did. He had not thought about that.

Himali and Himal.

Himal and Leslie.

Something was beginning to fall into place.

But he needed time to think about it.

Himal was now looking at him. When he recognized Peter, his voice changed. 'Uncle, what are you doing here?'

'He says he is a journalist,' said Himali. 'He said he wanted to take my interview.'

'He *is* a journalist,' said Himal. 'Leslie Uncle told me. He works for a famous newspaper.'

Himali's demeanour changed.

'Sorry, ahn Uncle, I thought you were just making me a fool. Come up now and sit, na.'

'No, no, no time now. Some other time...'

Peter made good his escape. Suddenly it seemed as if there was a link somewhere. But he didn't quite know where it was going. He took the train back and went to the police station.

'Can I speak to Leslie?' he asked.

'If you want, I will put in a word with the jail,' said Jende.

'I don't even need to go and meet him, I just want to ask him a question.'

'What question?'

'I want to know where his boarder was working.'

'Okay, that is not in the notes. You come tomorrow and you can talk to him on the phone.'

~

Only, the next morning it was Leslie who wanted to see Peter and Jende. His voice on the phone was angry and sharp and full of energy.

'You have to get me out of here, Peter,' he said. 'I didn't murder that young man. Or that child. You know it and everyone knows it. These kind men at the jail know it too and they've let me use their phone. Please come.'

Sunil asked if he wanted some lawyers' numbers.

'I think Jende will be enough,' Peter said.

When they arrived at Arthur Road Jail, Leslie was spitting with rage.

'There. Can you believe it? I am HIV negative. I mean I don't have the dread thing. They do the test here. I thought: why bother? I already know. But I'm so glad they insisted in their bureaucratic way and made me do it again and hey-nonny-nonny, I don't have the terrible thing,' the last few words were almost caroled in delight.

'You were so sure you did,' said Peter.

'Yes. I was. Can you imagine? Because of that little beast, Himal.'

Now things were becoming clear.

'He convinced me I should have the test. I didn't have a single symptom, but the beastie persuaded me I should and then he brought me the report and he said I must have given it to him as well so the least I could do was...'

'You were having relations with this man?' said Jende, his tone deliberately neutral.

'Oh my, now you can throw me back into the chokey for

admitting to unnatural sex, can't you? But yes, I was having relations with this man. If you can call a couple of blow jobs "having relations". I mean he wouldn't even allow me to kiss him. I told him it's only the ladies of the night who proscribe that sort of thing but he wouldn't listen. But what a body.'

Jende said nothing but Peter indicated to Leslie with his eyes that he might want to spare the Inspector's blushes.

'I see the delicacy of my position so I shall rein in the indelicacies. So the little tease tells me after what seems like days and days of prancing through the house in his underwear that he might agree to have something more to do with an old fossil if the said old fossil agrees to an AIDS test. And he says that he works in a path lab so he can do it and keep it private and so I agreed because, my dear, I was always so careful. I remember poor Ray, refusing to take anything except homoeopathy or something and just pretending that if he laughed a lot it would go away. And Mack got religion, poor thing, and went back into the arms of Mother Church, but I always say when no one is willing to have sex with you, that's easy, isn't it?'

Jende began to say something but Peter quelled him. 'So you agreed to an AIDS test?'

'Yes, indeed. I thought I could get it out of the way because you can't help wondering. I mean one good *choriso-pao* and I would be on the runs but now being on the runs is always: is this the beginning of the end? When does the Kaposi's sarcoma show up? Of course, they have loads and loads of pills now and everything is nearly all right but it is still something of a blight on one's social life, right? I mean, you have to hang out with other positive people, and my dear, they're almost all so completely in denial and so gung-ho and so we're-all-gonna-live-forever-in-a-yellow-submarine that I couldn't bear it, I just couldn't. And then there it was: I was HIV positive. But he did take me in his arms and comfort me...oh dear, the Inspector is blushing.'

Peter tried not to look at Jende but could tell he was discomfited.

'And the next morning, he was bringing me milk and saying that he was going to quit his job and take care of me because my virus count was so high. He said I should not have ignored it for so long if I knew and see how thin I had become and my dear Rock of the Ages, he persuaded me I was dying. Then he told me the most horrible story about his sister Himali and her husband Sooraj. Such an odd pair of names, no? I mean: all that ice would melt in the heat of the sun you would think.'

'What?'

For once Jende spoke. 'He's being clever, Pittr. Himali, ice. Sooraj even you would know. Sun.' And then Jende snorted and was quiet.

'Time enough to be clever later, Leslie. What did Himal tell you?'

'Oh it was quite a Greek tragedy, my dear, with the young man as a male Nemesis. You see, Himal had been saving up money to go abroad and make it big as the Queen of Queens, no, he wasn't really a queen. Anyway, he wanted to go abroad, to that overrated Apple, and then his mother fell ill. She had a kidney problem, I think. I would have thought a young man like him would have just scarpered but he was really devoted to his mother. So he took much of the money and put it in a joint account with his brother-in-law, who was quite fond of the old lady and wanted to contribute his share. Or he was in love with the said male Nemesis, I wouldn't be surprised. So they were going to buy her a new kidney. Quite reprehensible, I know, but apparently people do it all the time and the donor can live with one kidney, so they say. All of it was set up, the surgeon was lined up, some willing magic fingers from Serendib, and the operation theatre was booked and the donor had taken off his shirt and they'd painted a red X on his back—or her back, was it? I can't remember. Anyway, just when Maaji needed the dosh, it was gone. All of it. Poof. This Sooraj had been caught in the honey trap by that boy, Proxy, was that his name? Yes, Proxy. And those cops. They had blackmailed him and taken all the money. So Himal wanted to take revenge on all of them: on the boy who stood there, the cops who ran it, everyone. He wanted to get them all. And he had. He told me about how he went and killed the child, kindly, he said, because he knew how to do it clean and painless, being in the path lab and all. And then he told me how the father had gone mad and killed the other policeman. He didn't even have to kill the cops. They seem to have self-destructed. Guilt and rage. It's a potent combination, I think.'

'And that story about the clerk?'

'It's true. I loved and lost my little clerk and I couldn't do a thing about it. These men had been at it for years, making money out of the needs of others. I could do nothing for my beautiful Shwaas—that was his name, Shwaas. I offered him the money to shut them up when he told me what had happened. But he said no, he'd manage. And then he was gone. I think he gave them all that he'd saved for his family. And the shame was too much for him. I could only weep when I heard the news. I couldn't even go to his funeral. I couldn't even visit his grave because they cremated him and his ashes went off to Mother Ganga. So there was nothing left for me to mourn.'

Leslie stopped and asked for water but when a constable brought him a glass he waved it away. The moment passed and he could speak again.

'When Himal told me what he had done, I knew in my heart that it was what I should have done. I should have gone out and avenged my poor love. I should have come down like a wolf on the fold. Instead, I just sat around, making bad puns and eating violet creams. Himal seemed like such a warrior, as if he had gone out and fought the good fight for his mother and his brother-in-law. A life for a life in Hammurabi fashion,' he said and then becoming aware that his audience was not very sympathetic, he tried again: 'No, you have no idea how he told it to me. How much work he seemed to put into the revenge thing. First, he found out all the days on which Sooraj had made withdrawals. Then he used Sooraj's mobile phone and tracked down all the people who had called Sooraj on the days that he had made the payments and he found these two policemen. Then this boy Proxy. At first, he wanted to talk to Proxy and tell him how he had done something wrong, he said. But when he saw him in that toilet and realized that he was still up to his dirty tricks, he couldn't bear it any longer and he killed him, he said.'

'He just happened to be carrying a knife with him?'

There was a pause.

'I didn't think about that,' said Leslie, abashed.

'You didn't *want* to think about it,' said Jende.

Leslie shrugged slightly. 'Maybe. Maybe I was just blind. Maybe I wanted to be blind. But it seemed he expected it of me, expected me to take the fall for him. And then when he told me I had so little time, I thought I should do the right thing and take the blame.'

'The right thing?' Jende roared. 'You know how stupid this is? Is it the right thing to tell a lie? What would have happened if we had believed you then? What if we don't believe you now?'

Leslie's face crumpled.

'Oh dear, you are right. I am five kinds of a grass-green fool. And I don't even have the courage of my convictions. I mean if I thought it right when I thought I had AIDS, I don't know why I shouldn't think it right when I don't.'

Jende looked at him in disbelief: 'I don't know what you're talking but I will see what I can do.'

'Thank you,' said Leslie. 'Thank you so much. I don't know how to explain what happened. I don't even think I was in love. In lust, yes, but I know how to deal with that. I think it was his air of expecting one to do the best one could for him. As if he was entitled and you felt—okay, *I* felt—I felt not doing it for him would be as if one were letting down beauty itself. Beautiful people are like that, don't you find?'

Jende looked at him with such a complete lack of comprehension that Leslie changed track. 'Should I get a lawyer?'

'No,' said Jende. 'I will tell you if you need one. For the time being, we will simply drop the charges and let you go.'

Fifteen

They went back to Andheri, half-expecting to find the flat closed and the occupants missing. But the door was opened by Himal. He was only wearing a lungi and looked every inch the beautiful feral male.

Unprepared, Jende concealed his surprise with a frown. Then he took the lead.

'We are here investigating the murder of L.S. Parthusta, also known as Proxy.'

'Yes?' The liquid eyes went sharp and the jaw set tight.

'We have reason to believe that you might have information that you might want to share with us.'

'I thought you had already arrested Mr Leslie?'

'He will be released later today.'

'I see.'

It was obvious that Himal was going to play it cool. He kept his answers monosyllabic and to the point.

'Did you know the deceased?'

'No.'

'Did you have any contact with Sub-Inspector P.K. Durra or Sub-Inspector G.G. Pagmat?'

'No.' There was a small flicker in the eyes.

'Where were you on Sunday night?'

'I was with my sister.'

'Will she be willing to swear to this in a court of law?'

Himal smiled, a feline smile. 'Why won't she? It is the truth.'

'The truth will be decided in a court of law.'

'I am sure of it.'

There was a pause. Then Jende started again.

'Where do you work?'

'I am not working right now.'

'What was your last job? We believe you were with a pathology lab?'

'The Pathfinders Pathological Laboratories in Bandra.'

'What was your job there?'

'I was a lab assistant.'

'In what capacity did you work?'

'I took samples and gave injections to people in their homes.'

'And did you give insulin injections?'

There was no hesitation. 'To many people. Diabetes is a problem with many people.'

'Why did you stop working there?'

'I have lost my mother recently..'

'How did she die?'

'She was old.'

'Our information says she died in a hospital?'

'Yes.'

'Where you were organizing a kidney transplant for her?'

'We were taking her to Badama Hospital. The doctors there were treating her.'

'You had a considerable sum in a joint account with your brother-in-law, Sooraj Patel. What happened to it?'

A momentary hesitation now. 'You must ask him.'

'Your brother-in-law is dead.'

'And the answers are gone with him. So is my money. How am I to blame for this?'

'Was your brother-in-law being blackmailed?'

'I don't know. I only know that one day he killed himself and we found out that all the money I had saved was gone.'

'How much did you put into that account?'

'You seem to know. It was substantial.'

'How much did you earn at the Pathways Pathological Laboratories?'

'I don't think I have to tell you that.'

'I can find out easily.'

'Then I suggest you do that.'

It was obvious that the interview was going nowhere.

'I must ask you not to leave town and if you do, please notify me as to the address to which you will be going,'

Again, a flicker in those liquid eyes but it was quickly suppressed.

'I will do that.'

In the lift going down, Jende said: 'It is good. Now we know. It's him. He's the man. I could tell.'

'Intuition?'

'You call it what you want. There are people who kill. There are people who don't kill. Your friend? He doesn't kill. This one? Very easily.'

'Only...'

'Yes, don't say it. I know I cannot take my feelings to court. Now we need to build hard evidence. This will be easy. Once you have evidence, it will be easy.'

They began with the Pathways Pathological Laboratories. They did not have to work very hard at getting details of the salary Himal was being paid. The manager of the operation tried to hold out but Jende had only to say it was a murder investigation and that cooperation would ensure that the company's name would be kept out of the press, and all the details were forthcoming. Himal's salary was barely above subsistence, rather too small to merit paying guest accommodation in Bandra and to be contributing even a couple of lakhs to an account for his mother's treatment. And it was obvious he had enough money outside that for himself.

'Do you have a picture of this *banda*?' Jende asked.

The HR files were consulted and a photograph was found. Jende grunted in satisfaction because the man in the photograph was wearing the laboratory uniform.

'This will help people remember him.'

'Perhaps it would be better if he were to be shown in ordinary clothes,' Peter said.

'Enough,' said Jende impatiently. 'This is not one of your crime shows. This is Mumbai and we are the Mumbai Police. This is the way it happens here. You take a photo and you show and you say, "Is this the man you saw?" and if this is the man they saw, they say yes and if you say to them, "Will you swear to that in court?" they say "Court-kacheri? No baba, we will not go, because we are good people." One day one of these good people will need some witnesses and they will find that respectable people don't want to go to court for them either. Then it will serve them right.'

Peter saw that this was a hobby horse and Jende would be riding it off into the sunset.

'Now what?'

'Now we will go back to meet your friend, Himal Jugalkishore Shah.'

Himal greeted them without any change in expression.

'We know what you were earning at the Pathways Pathological Laboratory.'

'Oh?'

'How did you find this much money to save? I believe there was about four lakhs in just that one account. Even if half was yours, it's a lot to save in a few months.'

'I did side business.'

'What kind of side business?'

'I gave injections to people.'

'This you have told us. How much did you get for that?'

'One hundred rupees. One-fifty sometimes. Whatever people could pay.'

'You work a nine-hour shift and then you have time to go around the city giving so many injections?'

'My mother was ill. I had to work hard.'

'How did you feel when you found that the money was missing, this money you had worked so hard to make?'

'I was disappointed.'

'Disappointed?'

'Yes, disappointed.'

'If it were my mother,' said Peter, 'I would not just be disappointed. I would be angry.'

Himal stared at both of them. Then it was as if a dam had burst.

'Angry? You know the meaning of the word? *Chalo, theek hai*, I was angry. I was sad? Okay, I was sad. These are only words, Inspector. They don't explain what it is like when your mother is dying and you put your life aside to keep her alive and then you find someone has thrown all the money away. What will you say to her then? She is looking at you from the stretcher. She thinks you will save her. And up to that moment, you think you can save her. The doctor is ready. The hospital is ready. Only the money is gone. All gone.

'Some men might think: I should take revenge. I should kill the people who killed my mother, I should take from them what was taken from her. Eye for an eye, tooth for a tooth, kidney for a kidney. Some men might think like that. Some men might think: I should make them all suffer. But life is not like that, Inspector. Life is full of people who say: what is your degree? Why don't you do MBA? They will tell you to come to hotels for dinner with them but the next morning their secretaries will say they have gone abroad. Everyone gets these jobs but you have to make do with lab technician work. So you say, chalo, this is my fate and you tell yourself to carry on. And what do you find? You find that the police come and ask you questions. That is what you find. You know my neighbour, no? His name is Jotin Perry and he is a journalist. I am going to go and tell him that you are harassing me and I will ask him to put it in the papers. To put in the papers that you cannot do your own job so you send your friend to tell lies about fashion shoots and harass a woman who has just lost her husband and you mentally torture an honest, hardworking man who has just lost his mother. Now thank you so much for coming. I will show you the way out.'

Outside, Jende smiled.

'He has confessed. See, they always need to tell you what they have done.'

'No, he did not…'

'I know what he did not say and what he said. Even if he had said, "I killed that child, I slashed that man," I could not have used it. Confession to police will not be admitted in a court of law. But now that there is no doubt that he is the killer, we only have to find the evidence. Who did it is not so hard to find out, the difficult part is finding out how. You know that, Pittr. So go and ask your friend. How much was this *maa ka laadla* paying as rent? How did he get this money?'

~

Unfortunately, Leslie could not help them. Himal had agreed to pay the rent, never really meaning to pay, and Leslie had taken him in, never really expecting to be paid.

'He always said he would produce the rent, he only needed some more time,' said Leslie. 'It got to be rather a bore so I stopped asking. I just put it down to entertainment tax.'

Peter tried not to look askance.

'I know what you're thinking, Saint Peter of the Pearly Gates. But you have no idea how invisible one gets as one ages. He made me visible.'

Peter had no idea what to say to this.

'And yes, I gave him money too. It wasn't only the entertainment...How should I tell you this? There was—something incandescent about him that was irresistible. No, that's not the right word. I felt like he was a volcano, ready to explode but only I could keep him calm. That was such a compliment. There was a burning inside him, as if something was on fire.'

Pitale's words came back: look for rage.

Leslie cuddled a pillow to his face now.

'I am *so* glad to be back among my own things, Petey, you have no idea.'

'Serves you right for trying to be a hero.'

'You're telling me! I didn't expect jail to be quite so horrible. I mean, I didn't expect reality TV stars in the prison-look-of-the-year but it was smelly and boring. I thought I should ask to teach something, maybe conversational English or something, but I couldn't see myself as a teacher. I couldn't really see myself as a convict either; I couldn't actually see myself as anything except dying. And don't you dare say that we're all dying. I know we all are. But when it's closer, and someone keeps telling you that you're falling apart because these numbers are rising and those numbers are falling, you think: numbers don't lie, so I must be dying even if I'm feeling okay. You have no idea what it's like.'

As he sat there, talking to this unlikely figure in the dying light, Peter realized that Leslie might well be useful to the investigation. In a way, everything tracked back to the floating world of gay men, forced to meet in toilets and vulnerable to blackmail mainly because of an arcane law. Perhaps if he were to understand this world a little better...

'Leslie, do you think you could be part of the investigation?' he asked.

'I've told you all I know,' Leslie replied immediately but

there was a wary interest gleaming in those faded, shrewd eyes.

'I know that,' said Peter. 'But this case seems to have rather a lot to do with rough trade and...'

'And I, like Knowledge in the morality plays, am to go with you and be your guide through the dark underworld?' Leslie asked. 'It sounds utterly delightful. But I have to tell you, Peter my love, this will be a night-time job. Our world wakes up when the sun goes down. You're going to lose a lot of sleep.'

Peter's heart sank. He liked his sleep. He liked to be able to determine when and how much he got of it and when it began and when it ended and where he was going to get it. But he smiled and tried to look like this was what he had always wanted to do.

'When do you want to begin?' Peter asked.

'No time like the present,' said Leslie. 'Why don't you go home and get dressed nicely and meet me at the Churchgate Wheeler-dealer at eight pm?'

'What does dressed nicely mean?'

'I don't know. I don't think it would make much difference what you wore. But you could tuck your shirt in and comb your hair. Oh, and dark clothes, please.'

'Why dark clothes?'

'Camouflage, my love. Besides, black is the new pink in India.'

Peter did not know what this meant but sensing that it was a joke of some kind, he laughed.

At home, he told Millie where he was going and this time she seemed faintly amused.

'Do you know what your father's up to now?' she asked her son.

'I'm going to find out more about the gay world in Mumbai,' said Peter, looking his son in the eye. Sunil looked right back and smiled.

'Have fun, Dad.'

'Watch it, young man,' Peter wagged a finger at him. 'I'll need one of your shirts to wear. And call Uncle Shiva, tell him I need a copy of Himal Shah's photograph. I'll pick it up in twenty minutes.'

~

'Why Peter, how nice you look,' said Leslie, who was leaning against the A.H. Wheeler stall which sold newspapers, magazines, books and even a few railway miniatures.

'I had to borrow one of Sunil's black T-shirts,' he said. 'But really, why black?'

'Most of the places we're going are a bit open-air, if you know what I mean,' said Leslie as they walked down one of the platforms to the north end subway. 'So it's best to fit in. You don't want to be seen from afar.'

'Where are we going?'

'I thought we'd begin your tutorials with the mothership. This is where we all began our journey into Gayland: The yellow stone road. So let us go then, you and I, when the evening is spread out against the sky, like a patient etherized upon a table.'

They walked out into the sweaty night, and Peter followed Leslie past the empty Oval Maidan.

'This was also very much a hot spot. I've had such happy times here. My first seafood.'

'Surely not? Didn't you eat fish at home?'

'Oh my poor innocent Peter. I should explain. Seafood is gay slang for the sailorman. I suppose the vast majority hit port and make their way to the nearest red-light area. But some of them come to us. Maybe they're just gay in the first place. Maybe they've developed a taste for it from the life on the waves. I don't know. But that's what we call seafood.'

Peter looked over the flat expanse of the Oval.

'But where did you do anything?'

'Dear boy, you don't think we went all the way here, did you? This is where you find them and then you take them somewhere else.'

'And did you have to pay?'

'No. This was not about paying. It was not about love, of course. It was about lust. But in that way it was pure lust. It was about seeing something you liked and if it liked you, you took it home and had fun and it went away again. It was so clean, in a way, so clear, so free of all the noxious bits and pieces, the little nips and pinches that we inflict on each other in relationships. I almost never slept with the same guy twice.'

Peter had of course read all this when he was on the desk and editing copy on the AIDS pandemic. But it was different when he was being told this by a specific man who had done these specific things and made these specific choices.

'But there were also people who paid, no?'

'Oh there will always be people who pay. And the cynic would say you always pay. In one way or the other. But I suppose there are two types of paying transactions. One of them is when the deal is struck before anything starts. Someone begins to talk about money and after that everything runs smoothly if a figure is agreed upon. Those are what we call professionals. The other kind is when something begins to happen, or is in the middle of happening, and has happened and then the talk about money starts. Those we call cheaters.'

They were rounding the Regal and heading towards the Taj. The world was bright with people and taxis and young men with very large balloons, several feet across, and others selling musical instruments and maps. The Taj Mahal with its barriers and barricades, after the attack of 29/11, brought a temporary cessation of the noise and then they plunged into a street that Peter had walked many times before but was now completely transformed by night. The usual rush of people associated with a tourist spot such as this swirled around them: cotton candy man, chana-sing-wala, coffee-on-a-cycle, the astrologer and the seller of postcards. There were entire families squeaking and roaring at each other as they tried to squeeze the last moments of enjoyment out of an outing. There were couples leaning on the sea wall talking intensely to each other, their faces barely inches away, their breaths mingling, their worries monumental. There were also joggers and strollers and runners and power walkers. There were white people and brown people and black people.

But that wasn't it.

It was the peculiar quality of light that night brought to the street. No, he thought, no. It's the darkness. There is a deep darkness here, the darkness of the sea. And the light and the clamour of the land may fight it but it will lose. The sea is dark and the sea will win. A wave rose and fell and showed itself to have a fringe of light. Leslie settled himself on a free spot and patted the street next to him.

'If you're going to ask why this road, don't. I think it's because it was just next to Colaba and all the action was there in the bad old days. Some Ancient Ranis will tell you that it was the Arabs that did it.'

'Means?' Peter braced himself for something he didn't want to hear.

'Back in the day when the petrodollars started rolling in, the Arabs began to come to Bombay for the rains. And the Taj was spectacularly placed for them to watch the clouds roll in. I had a friend here who told me that they were always throwing open the windows, just to enjoy the rain, and over-stressing the air-conditioning. And of course since some of them liked a little on the side, there would be local talent waving and calling from the street below.'

Peter looked around and tried to imagine it.

'Didn't the police clear them away?'

'I don't know about that. I wasn't here. I'm telling you what I heard. But maybe that's why Voodoo and Gokul's became such gay hang-outs but I'm not sure about all this. I was a Bandra Queen and this was south of the border, down Mexico way for me.'

There was a moment of silence.

'Now tell me what it is we're looking for.'

'More on Himal.'

'I could tell you some.'

'Go on then.'

'Not like that, Peter. Ask me specific questions.'

'Is he gay?'

'Is that a specific question? I suppose it is, where you come from.'

'Is that an answer?'

'Peter, you're getting a little too smart for your heteroboots. Okay, there are men who want to get their way in the world, male Becky Sharps. Now all of us make some compromises, right? I wanted to be a writer but I ended up a copywriter. Some men draw a line here: I won't be a sycophant. Some draw a line there: I won't use my body. Some are so committed to what they want that they will do what it takes to get where they want. Himal is one of those. He has a body and he will use it because it is easier and faster than using his mind, which, I noticed, isn't entirely ordinary, but he's in a hurry.'

'What do you think it is that Himal wants?'

'The same thing everyone of his generation wants. They want what they call lifestyle. I mean, at one time this kind of boy wanted a Benetton shirt and VIP Y-fronts. Today they want to buy their suits in Singapore and they want Calvin Klein *chuddis*. And that's only the clothes. Multiply the demands: the right flat in the right area, the car or the

SUV or the car *and* the SUV, the smart phone, and you can see why they're always trying to trade up. The old way was the education way but that isn't one that everyone can use. What if you're just not up to the study and sum-up route? What if your brain has played you false? Or you didn't get enough potassium in your early days? What if, on the other hand, you have a nice body and you think you can use that to get somewhere in the world? Why not use it?'

A man of a certain age with a somewhat improbable quiff came up and said, 'Leslie! What are you doing here? I thought you had found true love?'

'Oh, it's a cryin' shame.'

'We don't have it no more? What happened?'

'It's a long story.'

'I like them long. Who's your friend?'

'Hi, I'm Peter Fernandes,' said Peter.

'I'm The Fonz,' said the man and then looking at Leslie, 'Does he know Virginia?'

'Oh, is that old one still doing the rounds?' Leslie asked. 'No, he doesn't know Virginia.'

'Gosh, Virginia goes unknown these days,' and almost as quickly as The Fonz had materialized, he lost interest and drifted off.

'Who's Virginia?' Peter asked.

'Code,' said Leslie. 'He didn't know you and wanted to know if you were gay. Since he couldn't ask me openly in front of you, he says, "Does he know Virginia?" And if you're not, I only have to say, "No, he doesn't" and no one is any the wiser. In my time, we used to say, "Does he know Earnest?" because of Oscar Wilde, you know, and how he ended his magnificent play on that little code line of his, of how important it was to know Earnest.'

There seemed to be much to learn. At the newspaper where he worked, the desk had often mocked a line that the reporters threw around: 'It's a subculture we know nothing about,' they would say and the desk loved the air of self-importance and sanctimonious piety with which the reporters declaimed their own ignorance. But here indeed was just that subculture, one he knew nothing about.

'Now what?' he asked Leslie.

'Now we wait. The gay life I know is about waiting. First you wait for the sun to go down. Then you wait for the meerkats to pop out of their holes and sniff around. Then you wait for someone to notice you. Then you wait for him to make the first move. The mating's about the waiting.'

'Don't you ever make the first move?'

'In extremis, my love, only in extremis.'

Peter did not ask.

Time passed slowly. Leslie pointed out the notables of his world: The Photographer, so called because he came to watch and seemed to be able to absorb everything through his eyes; Iggie, because of a white patch in his hair; Rocket, who took people back to a room in Grant Road and then when they were nude, ripped a hole in their shirts and threatened to do the same to their trousers if he were not given as much money as he asked for.

'Can we talk to him?'

'My dear, you may try. I am certainly not going to.'

'I need someone to introduce me,' Peter said.

The Fonz came by again.

'Fonzie, my boy here wants to meet the Rocket.'

'Why?'

'He's got a little research.'

'Is that what they're calling it these days?'

'Yes or no?'

'Oh well, if I must. Come on then. But I won't be seen talking to him myself. I'll introduce you and be off. Do you have a *nom de guerre*?'

'No, he's in no need.'

'Why a nom de guerre?'

'Generally everyone takes a name in the game,' said The Fonz. 'It becomes easy if you're always called the same thing.'

'Like The Fonz?'

'No,' snapped The Fonz. 'That's my real name.'

Rocket was lounging in a dark spot where the road by the sea snaked off past the Radio Club and became a morass of perfume stores, restaurants and cheap hotels.

'Rocket, this is Peter,' said The Fonz. 'And vice versa.'

'Nice name, Peter,' said Rocket and flicked something on his phone. The phone had a flashlight which he allowed to play over his face.

'Don't,' said The Fonz. 'I told you. That makes you look like a *bhoot*.'

Indeed, it did, lighting him up from beneath, throwing wild shadows from his cut-glass cheekbones on to the sockets of his eyes. The boy shrugged and switched it off.

'And he's not a client,' said The Fonz.

Rocket lost interest immediately.

'*Dhande ka time hai. Dimaag ka dahi mat banaa*. Time is money.'

'I'll pay,' said Peter, uncomfortably aware that he had no idea how much the going rate was. He turned to look at The Fonz for guidance but he had made one of his quick disappearances.

'For what will you pay?' Rocket asked, in English this time, a strange English in which American, British and Educated Indian struggled for supremacy.

'For information.'

'On what? For what?'

'There was a murder in the toilet in Matunga Road...'

'Proxy, na? *Chutiya tha. Police ka tattu*. One day someone was going to take him. I warned him first only. I said: don't do this. Go with them. Or don't go with them. These policewala *haraamis* won't save you when there is bad trouble.'

'But you also take them to a room and tear their shirts.'

'Who told you this lie?' Rocket looked outraged. 'That is why you're scared, Uncle? That is why? Don't worry. I'll look after you. *Nas-nas khol doonga, saahab*. Tottal heppiness.' His voice had turned wheedling.

Peter wanted to say, 'I'm not like that,' but he remembered Unit's savage response. So he said, 'Did you know Proxy?'

'I know each one, from the *santri* to the *mantri*. Yes, I knew him. He was a tattu. The other one is the tough one. That one, Unit. I know him well.'

'Unit?'

'*Poochh na mereko, poochh*. I know each one of these people. How they are from the outside is not how they are from the inside. Some are all muscles and tight-tight T-shirts and they walk like they're Tarzan in his *langot*. But when two dogs are fighting, they cross the road. Unit? He's not like that. One day, this banda Proxy, he thought he'll do it alone, okay? He'll go to the toilet and he'll get the guy and then he can take everything instead of sharing with the police. So he goes and he stands and he shakes and shakes until it comes up. Next to him one boy comes, ahn? Thin and yellow type. He is in good clothes, American style: jeans, T-shirt. When this banda reaches out, Proxy grabs his hand and says, "*Chal police thane*." But that boy is doing this mix martial art. He is giving Proxy one kick like this and one fight like that,' and here Rocket lashed out with the high style of a Bollywood street fighter. 'Proxy is running and after him, that Mix Martial Art is running. This is a North-Eastern fucker and they can hit, those boys! Like steel wire, they are. He would have finished Proxy right there, but outside there is Unit. On the platform of the station. Means, he doesn't know fighting, like. But he just comes in the way and he throws his body, *phataak*, like that, straight at this boy. They fought and it only stopped when that Unit's head got broken. That mark, na—on his forehead?—he got it from that only.'

Peter remembered the scar. It had looked too fresh to belong to childhood.

'Unit has guts. But Proxy? You know what he did? He just left his friend and he ran. That kind he was. Don't bother with this *chootmaarike*. If he died, it is good for everyone. Even for that Unit. Now I have to go. Time is money.'

'Of course,' Peter said. 'Just one more thing.' He pulled out Himal's photograph. 'Do you know him?'

Rocket took a quick look. 'Arre, Daddy, big *shaukeen* you are. This one looks expensive.'

'He may know something about the murder. I need some background. Used to work at a path lab in Bandra. Pathfinders.'

'That will be extra. Two thousand, okay? And I'm doing it only because I don't like *lafda* in our business. Proxy was a *chutiya* but killing is not allowed.'

'Two thousand is fine,' Peter said, hoping Jende wouldn't bite his head off if this came to nothing.

'The banda looks familiar, but I'm not sure. Give me the photo, I'll ask the others. Come back tomorrow. And five hundred for today.'

Peter gave him the money and he winked and was gone like a rocket.

Sixteen

Jende had spent the day trying to track down Himal's life before Mumbai. He had not had much luck.

'He did not do much in Surat. Went to college, did not even get into student politics. If he had, we would have a file.'

'Why?'

'Because there is always a file,' said Jende. 'Before, these student unions were big trouble. There would be Sec 363 or Sec 503...'

'Means?'

'Sec 363 is for Kidnapping and 503 is for Intimidation. Today it has cooled down a bit in the big cities but in the small towns, it is all very much there and the political parties give money for *lafda*, fights. But he has done nothing. No police record.'

They were walking around the park.

'So what are you going to do?'

'I am going to finger.'

'Again?'

'Again. You also come.'

Peter did not have much else to do by day and so they went back to see Himal. He seemed to be about to go to sleep when they arrived.

'Inspector,' he said. 'Come in.'

'We have come to meet your sister.'

'She is not in the house.'

'We will wait until she comes back.'

Himali appeared behind her brother's shoulder.

'What are they doing here?'

Himal turned and snapped at her in Gujarati.

'*Gaandi*, better they come in. Do you want the whole neighbourhood knowing police are at the door? Come in, Inspector. Do you want tea?'

'No thank you.'

'I'm going to sleep,' Himal said.

'Haan, stay out all night then you sleep all day,' Himali said.

'*Shaanti raakh*,' snapped Himal and slammed into the bedroom.

'Does your brother go out at night?'

'He's a young man,' said Himali. 'He's unmarried. He has a social life.'

'He does not have a job.'

'I'm so unlucky. Other women, they get married and they don't have to think about money. My husband dies. Now my brother does not have a job.'

'But he has a lifestyle, still?'

'I don't ask him and he doesn't ask me,' she said.

'You don't have a job. He doesn't have a job. How come you're still living in this flat and paying rent and cable and electricity and everything?'

'I don't know,' said Himali and then her voice took on an almost hysterical note. '*I don't know*. You ask him, no? He has money. He always has money.'

And she put her head into her *dupatta* and began to weep. Jende gestured to Peter and they slipped out quietly.

'This boy is earning money somehow,' said Jende. 'He's getting money from somewhere. And she thinks it is not a good place, from where it is coming.'

'Did you get his bank records?'

'I did but there's nothing there. But then what bad money is going through the bank? Every child knows that if it is black, you keep it at home, not in the bank.'

Peter yawned. He wanted a nap. Late nights did not agree with him now and he was up for another night out with Leslie.

'Achha, I'll need another copy of Himal's photo,' he said.

'You're making an album of the fellow or what? Theek hai. I'll tell Zurale to get you another copy.'

'Why don't you get Zurale to follow Himal?'

'You are reading too many of those crime books,' said Jende. 'You think it is easy to spare two men from duty and send them out to follow someone? I have to explain why all the overtime.'

He looked suspiciously at Peter.

'And please, aahn, you don't get any ideas about following him yourself. Otherwise Millie-bhagat will be knocking on my door.'

Peter grinned reluctantly and went home to lunch. He wanted desperately to nap but Millie would have none of it.

'Never from bed to board or board to bed.'

She made him help her sort out some sheets and turn over the mattresses and when she thought a sufficient amount of time had elapsed, she let him lie down. Peter thought he was going to sleep immediately but while his body felt the intense internal pressures of fatigue, his eyes remained open.

Millie lay down next to him.

'Are you still thinking about that disgusting murder?' she asked.

'Precisely because it is disgusting,' he said. 'And murders now, not a murder.'

'Tell,' she said and turned on her side, facing him and giving him her entire attention. He brought her up to date and when he told her how he felt stymied by Himal, she had a solution.

'Go and talk to the people who work with him,' she said. 'They might give you some ideas.'

~

It required a phone call from Jende to the human resources manager at the Pathfinders Pathological Laboratories to get Peter access to the three laboratory assistants in their employ, two men and a woman. And although both the management and the assistants tried to build up what they did, Peter soon realized that they actually only fetched and carried samples from those who were too infirm or ill to come to the laboratories. They rarely if ever did anything clinical, that being left to the pathologists and the clinicians. The boys were Jaywant and Radhakrishna; the woman was Suruchi. She had been hired to replace Himal and so had nothing to say about him.

'He was about to be thrown out,' said Jaywant. 'He was not on time, he was always going to sleep, like he had been up all night.'

'Haan, he was out in the night,' said Radhakrishna. 'Once I was going to Bandra very late and he was at the station, like waiting for someone.'

'Platform one?' asked Jaywant.

Radhakrishna smirked.

'There is waiting and there is waiting,' said Jaywant gnomically.

'He was doing other kinds of work?' Peter asked. 'Night work?'

He tried to make his voice suggestive but it had an involuntarily chilling effect. The young men looked at each other and as if by a signal, withdrew into themselves and began to deny any knowledge of anything out of the way. Peter cast about for another tack.

'Himal said that he gave lots of injections,' he said. 'He said he gave insulin injections to many patients.'

Again the quick look, guilty, scared.

'It's okay, I know all about it,' said Peter, taking a chance.

'See, sirji, if a nurse comes to your home to give you an injection, she will charge a professional rate. Many people cannot afford that,' Jaywant explained.

'*Bas, haan*?' Radhakrishna interrupted him. 'Not that they can't afford but they don't want to afford. What is this afford-shafford when it comes to health? But people are like that. They will pay for coffee but not for a nurse.'

'His to-be is a nurse so he's talking big. You see, sirji, when the patient has sugar that is very high, we know. We see that the doctor will say insulin injections and some people cannot afford to come regularly to the lab or a doctor or afford a nurse, so we say, we will come for less money and give the shot. It's the same thing. And we go.'

'So do you buy the insulin?'

'Now everything is on prescription. You can't get even a headache without a prescription. Where will we get prescriptions? Patient or family have to buy and keep the insulin at home, we only go to give injections.'

'How does it work? You have fixed clients?'

'Nothing like that. We have ten clients between three of us—actually two and a half, because that Himal would often not show up and now this Suruchi is newly married lady and has her *majboori*, you see.'

Peter said he saw.

'So whoever can go, goes. That way no one finds out. Because these clinicians and pathologists and doctors are all united, they will tell the patients, don't let anyone come. Arre, are we just anyone? They want to fleece people and keep everything for themselves. Maximum profit. They exploit.'

Peter nodded understandingly.

'These people don't want others to come up,' Jaywant continued, growing expansive. 'We offer good service. Even if people don't have insulin at home, we can get it. Because this shirt is like our ID,' he said, pointing to the patch on his pocket. 'We go next door to Good Health Chemists and they give what we ask for, and no questions because they know where we work. We're going to take these medicines and sell or what?'

Peter wondered whether Himal had gone and bought any insulin. He had used what he had found in the fridge at the Durra home but he could not have been sure there would be enough there to kill the child.

He went next door to the Good Health Chemist with Himal's photograph and struck gold. A somewhat crotchety middle-aged woman was sitting behind the counter and remembered Himal coming to buy insulin.

'Why do you want to know?'

'I'm working with the police, this is related to a murder they're investigating.'

The woman looked unconvinced. Peter called Jende on his phone and explained the situation.

'Give her the phone,' said Jende. Peter handed the woman his mobile. After two minutes, during which the woman listened with interest, the matter was sorted.

'He rarely came,' she said, handing Peter his phone. 'The other two came regularly. One day he came and asked for six doses. I gave them to him because Pathfinders is always sending the boys for this or that and sending the prescription later. I gave them to him, on...one minute, let me tell you.'

She dug about in a drawer and pulled out an old book of counterfoils, over which carbon paper smears seemed to be the prevalent pattern.

'Haan, here it is.'

The dates matched. The insulin had been bought on the morning that the child was murdered.

'How do you remember this sale so clearly?' he asked.

'Because he came that evening and gave them back. I had to cancel the transaction and give his money back.'

'Goods once sold…?'

'You can do all that in any other shop. But for chemists, the government has different rules. You can say if you are in a cloth shop: these shirts come in packs of three, take all three or go somewhere else. You cannot say that in a chemist's shop. If they ask for one, you have to give one. If they ask for two, you have to give two. About returns, no one is sure. Some say we shouldn't take it back. Some say, why bother, take it back before they make a scene. Because sometimes we can't tell what the doctor's handwriting says and we ask, "This is for head? This is for stomach?" and we give by guessing. If it is the wrong medicine or the wrong quantity, better to take it back. This boy came back with the insulin and he said, "No need" and I said, "Next time I will not give" and he said, "Arre don't worry about next time, Auntie," and he took his money.'

Gotcha, thought Peter.

Seventeen

'Just ask Himali if she has diabetes or a blood sugar problem,' Peter told Jende.

'She will say she is an innocent widow, how can she have such problems?' Jende said mournfully.

Peter chuckled. 'I know, but now we have him in the chemist's shop on the day the boy died. We have him buying insulin and returning it. The woman at the chemist's shop remembers him. We have him at the home of the child—that lab uniform should be sufficient evidence, no? And perhaps the boy's mother will also remember him now. Then we have motive and we have opportunity.'

'All circumstantial and he has an alibi, remember?'

'The sister?'

'She will say what she needs to say. He has told her: I was at home. She will say: he was at home. This is the problem with families. They will say what you want them to say.'

'But everyone knows that. The judge also knows that.'

'And then it depends on the judge. I don't want to depend on the judge. I don't want to go looking for a judge who will accept this. I want proof and there is no proof.'

Peter tried not to feel as if he were responsible for this state of affairs. There was only one person he hadn't gone back to yet for further clues, a man who knew at least one of the dead men, perhaps three: the senior Pagmat. And so it was to his house that Peter went.

The household help was as surly, the old man as desiccated.

'Why have you come?' the old man asked. 'They are all dead. This is the way of the world. They say na: *neki kar aur dariya mein daal*? But what if the lake is a gutter? And what if the gutter starts in your house?'

There was no answering this. 'How are you?' he asked instead.

'How will I be? I am eighty-eight years old. Now the boys I taught say: Pagmat Sir is *alive*? On my eightieth birthday they came, ten-twenty of them. They brought cake and wafers and Fanta. They knew I liked Fanta.'

'Fanta-Shanta the old man wants,' said the household help, walking through the room with a broom and a dust-pan.

'Sattu!' the old man shrieked.

'Drink and die,' said Sattu.

Senior Pagmat turned to Peter again. 'They took pictures and I said I hope I will hit a century. At that time, I meant it too. I could do twelve surya namaskars, properly, not like they're teaching in school today, making a joke of yoga. And I walked to Shivaji Park before I walked around it; no sitting on the *katta* and talking to old men. Good walking, fast walking, and then home for light breakfast. Nothing is left. Now no walking, nothing.'

'No relatives also,' said Sattu.

This time the old man ignored him.

'They tell me my nephew was doing bad things. That he was taking these boys and making them do bad things. To blackmail people. That is not what we taught him. This he learned somewhere else. Where did he learn these things?'

Peter remained silent.

'So many boys came here to take bath. In school, I could pick them out, they were so clean because they came here. Water, soap. If they hadn't cleaned their teeth I gave them *dant manjan*.'

'Do you remember Proxy?'

'Lachhman?'

'Yes, Lachhman Parthusta.'

'I remember each one. He was killed, you came to ask about him before. I remember everything, nothing wrong with my memory. Only this body...That Lachhman could bowl but he could not bat. He could not face the fast bowlers. It was okay with tennis ball or rubber ball but once he got hit with a season ball and *bus*. He was shaking. He would sweat so much, the salt would burn his eyes. But he was good at kabaddi.'

Peter wondered whether he was going to get anything beyond a Physical Education Teacher's reminiscences.

'There was also one called Unit.'

'His father was a drunkard, always coming and telling us he would take him out of school and put him to work in a *bhatti*. He worked in one himself. He distilled. For one of the aunties.'

Peter did a quick calculation.

'Prohibition must have ended many years before, no?'

'Where do I know anything about all this? But they tell me that once you get a taste for hooch, you can't go back. Everything else is *pheeka*.'

'Was Unit a good player?'

'No. No control. Anyone could make him do anything. Take kabaddi. Your breath goes, you go back. But one person in the opposite team had to say, "Ay *darpok*" or "See how he's going with his tail between his legs" and he would turn around immediately and go back. And then he would be caught. One insult and he would lose his temper and he would hit. Then he did not see if the boy was big or small or what. He would just hit.'

Sattu brought tea. '*Ek-ek*,' he said with a delighted mournfulness. 'One by one, they're going.'

'Only I am here,' said Pagmat Senior, and then, 'This tea has no taste.'

'Your tongue has no taste.'

'My tongue is fine. See?' He stuck out his tongue.

Peter drank his lukewarm tea—the old man was right, it had no taste—and made good his departure. On his way out he tipped the household help.

'Anything you want to know, you ask me,' Sattu said.

'Did Inspector Pagmat leave anything here?'

Sattu smiled a small discreet smile. Then he reached into his banian and brought out a key. 'This.'

When Jende came to take charge of the key and process it as evidence, the atmosphere in the room had changed to one of sullen anger. The general feeling was of being let down. Sattu had expected to be let into the treasure which he was sure was in a locker somewhere.

'Now it is gone,' he said.

'Police will take charge of it,' said Jende.

'Everyone knows what that means.'

'What does that mean?'

'Arre, forget it, why should I say? It will be the lathi for me.'

'Look, look, what a world we live in!' cackled the old man. 'This is money he earned by dirty deeds. Now this one is worried that it will go to the police who will rob it. Who is robbing and who is robbed?'

Jende allowed himself a rare smile.

'You can come along, Kaka,' he said. 'Come with us when we open the locker.'

'It is a locker? A bank locker?' Sattu looked like he was going to burst out of his clothes.

'Yes. You also come.'

'If I come, he has to come,' said Pagmat. 'He carries me.'

'*Yeh bojh hai roj ka*,' said Sattu. He sounded like it was

a line he had tried in his head for years before he had got an opportunity to say it aloud. He brought a wheelchair from the other room and lifted the old man into it, refusing help from Jende and Peter.

They made a strange group around the locker in the cold, dry vault in the basement of the bank. There were two keys, one of them held by the bank and one by the owner. There was also a password but Jende's presence, with a receipt book, allowed them to pass over that.

The locker had two bags in it. They were filled with bank notes, thousand-rupee notes. Sattu looked at the bags and his eyes filled with greed and horror.

'If I knew English, na,' he said, 'this would be my money.'

'And why is that?' Pagmat Senior asked. 'You were his son?'

'I had the key.'

'This is the piggy bank saying it owns the money.'

Jende shrugged.

'It is now police property,' he said. A teller was called and sworn in and made to count the money as Peter filmed it on his phone. It amounted to four and a half lakhs.

~

Sunil was at home when Peter returned.

'Oh, Unit called. He wanted to talk to you,' Sunil said.

'I'll call him later,' Peter replied. 'I'm going to take a nap. I have to go out again with Leslie tonight.'

Sunil looked up from his laptop and made as if to say something, then decided on silence and went back to his typing.

Peter went into the bedroom and closed the door. His body felt thick with age and fatigue. When he had undressed and crawled into bed, the sun slipped through the curtains and dappled a triangular area on the covers near him. He moved his hand into the sun and enjoyed the warmth for a moment and let his body relax totally. This was the glory of retirement, he thought, that one could take afternoon naps and not feel guilty.

But when he woke up, several hours later, his mouth was full of fur, his brain was coated in wool and he had dribbled on his pillow. This is the glory of old age, he thought, it takes several days to recover from a single night out, and another one's coming up.

He thought about calling up Leslie and cancelling but then he conjured up that pathetic body in the Matunga Road station toilet, the image of the child lying limp in Jende's arms, the mess of brain and bone and blood that Durra left behind. He would go because he might chance upon something more about this case, about those toilets, something that would seal Himal's fate. Perhaps he might also learn something about a life that Sunil may have chosen. Or not. Would he ever know?

He dragged himself into the bathroom and had a bucket bath. He never used more than one, careful not to waste water. But now, he finished his bath by pouring half a bucket over his head, hoping the small torrent would shock his body out of exhaustion.

~

Leslie had said they would meet at Bandra, under the eaves, 'where men are adamant about Eve dropping'. Peter had groaned politely. The pun was one of Leslie's many tricks, some linguistic, some expressed in clothes and some in the body. Sometimes, Peter thought, the tricks become the self. Leslie seemed like a hall of mirrors, constantly reflected, echoed, each one being checked against some standard that had nothing to do with who he really was. 'Leslie fatigue,' he said aloud to himself. 'I have Leslie fatigue.'

The station was bright with people and activity. It seemed as if everyone was in constant motion, a Bombay phenomenon. It reminded him of what an old Goan aunt who had come to see him had said about the city: 'Everyone looks as if they're going to collide and then they veer away at the last minute.' How could there be a sex market here?

'Don't be silly, dear,' said Leslie. 'You've got into this the wrong way. It's all those cheats and rent boys and honey traps filling your mind. It's not a market so much as a singles bar. Most of these men are simply here to get some sex.'

'But where?'

'Ah, that's the question. Say this city has ten million souls, ten have bedrooms, the rest don't even have holes. Oh dear, that didn't sound too nice. We all have holes, don't we? But as I was saying, there's no room in the city for love. Not even for the hetters. So what do we do? We do it in toilets, standing next to each other, and that's how the police get at us. And the cheats. And now the maniacs with the knives. But that's how it works when you pile all these hundreds of thousands of men in the city without women.'

'You're saying it's situational?'

'I would love to believe that all these men want to have sex with other men out of choice. But that's when I'm fantasizing. I know otherwise: we're sexual beings and we need sex in one way or the other. A lot of the men who come here aren't necessarily looking for other men. A hole warm and willing is what they want, or that is what they tell you.'

'Unit was saying that everyone says: I'm not like that.'

'They do. But what do they mean? Do they mean I'm not the kind who approaches young men in toilets, young men who are obviously on sale? Do they mean I'm not the kind who approaches men at all, of whatever kind? I don't think they know. I think they're rejecting being gay, they're rejecting camp because that's the only image they have of being gay, they're rejecting outsider status and they're desperate to keep their footing in the world they know, the safe heterosexual world, even as they take one more step towards the edge.'

Peter felt deeply sad.

'Was that how it was for you?'

'No,' said Leslie. 'I knew. I knew when I was eight or something. I knew I wanted to see men nude. I think that was about it, at the time. My poor Papa, he had such hopes for me because I wanted him to buy me those muscle magazines, you know, the ones with all those men in the tantalizing little trunks. No, I'm not a Muscle Mary now but at the time, my dear, where else could you begin to guess what other men had?'

'By looking at yourself?'

'Oh rubbish. That's narcissism. I never suffered from that. Now look at the young man there, he's been walking up and down for nearly five minutes. He's one of the tribe. Don't gawk, dear, he'll think you're interested.'

'How do you know?'

'He's glittering.'

'What does that mean?'

'I think it has something to do with how one walks, how one holds oneself, where one stops, what one looks at. It's in the eyes generally. The quick glance that takes in your face and body, the more pointed glance at your genitals, that's a kind of signal I suppose, and then back to the eyes to see if you've noticed that one's been looking and to see what you think of the looking. If you're blank, one cuts away quickly as if one didn't mean anything. But if there's any interest and you linger despite the body scan, things are headed somewhere. That's why it's easier in the toilet.'

'That's because?'

'Because most people just do their business in one of our stinky loos and get the hell out of there. But if you're willing to stay, if you're there while the men come and go, then it's obvious you're like Michelangelo. This is an advanced class: How to spot a gay man at ten paces without the help of tincture of urea.'

And slowly, with Leslie's aid, Peter began to pick out the men who waited and headed to each other, slowly, had brief exchanges and drifted apart again or in some cases, left together. Leslie was right; many of them seemed like middle-class men, the bank teller, the insurance broker, the car salesman. The younger men seemed to be either college students or young men dressed to look like college students.

'Rani Maa!' said a young man in white jeans and a Navy cap, coming up to Leslie and bowing as if he were a cavalier in a costume drama. 'What brings you out of the dower house?'

'The call of duty,' said Leslie. 'It's a clear call and a wild call that will not be denied.'

'Ooh, poetry. I love poetry. Why I dropped out of Eng lit for math. Did you know?'

This was said to Peter, who wondered why he should.

A man walked past them and said briefly, without inflection, without haste, 'Police.'

'As if they're going to bother us just because we're standing here,' said the young man.

'This is Rahul,' said Leslie. 'They're all called Rahul.'

'Why?' asked Peter.

'Doesn't he know Virginia?' the young man asked.

'Does he look like he's fit to know Virginia?'

'Oh, a tourist. Why doesn't he stay and join the club? I'm so tired of them calling us a minority, I'd admit anyone into the ranks. Like one of those signature campaigns where people sign up to save the whales when they couldn't care about whales.'

It was obvious to Peter that no one was going to tell him why gay men in the city chose Rahul as a pseudonym.

Another man passed by and said, ‘Police.’

‘It’s an epidemic of warnings,’ said Rahul. ‘I should go and see.’

He was back in a moment, his face worried, his manner business-like.

‘They’re rounding up people for questioning. Known offenders, they’re calling it. All the rent boys and chicken hawks and everyone. Go then, Rani Maa, go home. I’m turning in too.’

Eighteen

The news spread as if by jungle drums. Nothing happened. No mad rush; just a steady leaking away. Peter caught a train southwards, wondering if anyone had thought he was part of the exodus. After all, he had been speaking to Leslie and to 'Rahul'. Odd, he thought, odd, how much we worry about what others will think of us.

And then Peter's phone beeped in his pocket. Jende had sent him a message:

'Cm 2 Mtnga Rd stn.1 more.'

No. Not Unit, prayed Peter, not Unit. He knew better than to call Jende up; he would be in the thick of the crisis that every dead body brought with it.

On the train Peter fought the panic building up inside him. 'Why do you think it might be Unit?' he asked himself. 'He had nothing to do with the blackmail. Sooraj wouldn't have had his number on his phone. No, it can't be him.' But the dread remained. He was the only one left with a connection to Proxy, after all. He'd kept Proxy's money.

He got off at Matunga Road Station and made his way to the north end of the platform. The same knot of people seemed to be there, the same gawking men, the same questions, the same assumptions. More than one person fell off a train every day in this city or died while crossing the tracks; the assumption was that it would be one of these. Perhaps even an important person to merit such attention.

Otherwise it would be a pair of orderlies, a stretcher and a spotty sheet covering the body as it was rushed away to the city morgue.

Jende was standing in the middle of it all, an oasis of silence and rage.

He pointed into the toilet and Peter went in, braced and ready.

Only, it wasn't Unit sprawled on the floor of the toilet, it was Himal. The beautiful animal body of which he had taken so much care was despoiled. He had died as Proxy had died, a slash to the side. There was something else as well, something that linked the young man to Proxy but in the middle of the blood and gore and piss, he could not tell what it was.

Peter stumbled out into the night.

'What happened?'

Jende shrugged but it was not inflected with a lack of caring as shrugs are. This was a shrug that said your guess is as good as mine and both our guesses are a complete waste of time.

'Has a body part been taken?' Even as he said this, Peter knew it was stupid.

'Yes, I put my hand inside and tried to find out what was there and what was not.'

'Sorry,' said Peter. Jende grunted. Then a moment later, he said, 'Sorry. I will tell them to check for that as well.'

'Should we be telling his sister?'

'We need a lady officer to come with us at this time of the night. When she gets here, we will go. Tea?'

They walked together to the tea stall in the middle of the station. As usual Peter ordered tea and paid for it. If Jende did this, there would be a ritual battle in which the tea stall owner would tell him that of course he didn't have to pay and Jende would say that he certainly had to. Once Peter had asked him why he did this. 'Isn't it easier to just take the tea? Or is it a matter of principle?' Jende laughed a little. 'You remember Saul's?' How could Peter forget? Saul's was a small stall by the sea, set up as a cooperative endeavour by the class of 1970 of St Peter's, the school to which Peter and Jende would both later go. Almost the entire class had contributed a hundred rupees each when Saul, ace athlete, academic disaster area, hail fellow well met, had broken his legs jumping off the Vashi Bridge. 'I was at the back when two police came in and ordered something, noodles and garlic chicken dry or something,' Jende said. 'When the order was finished, the cook did aakh-thoo, as if he were spitting in the food and the waiter did aakh-thoo. Maybe sometimes they spat as well, who knows? Because the police didn't pay. So from then on I pay. Otherwise, they spit in your food. Maybe not really but in their heads, certainly.'

Now they sipped the oversweet tea until their chaperone turned up and could escort them to Andheri. But Sub-Inspector Jayshree Patil too wanted a cup of tea because she was tired, having been on duty at a temple, frisking female devotees. Peter was about to go up when she took it upon herself to order and to ignore the niceties of payment. Meanwhile time ticked steadily on. Peter could see the signs of restlessness in Jende and he suggested quietly that they phone Himali and warn her of their arrival.

'Is that a good idea?' Jende asked the air.

'Better than going there in the middle of the night and saying your brother is dead.'

'I am saying we should go in the morning only,' said Patil.

'By the morning she will be at a police station saying her brother is missing and then if she finds out we had the body and we did not inform her, she will go straight to the papers to say Mumbai police are like this, Mumbai police are like that.'

'That is there,' said Patil.

It was almost midnight before they set out for the housing society.

'You don't think she killed him, do you? I mean, men's toilet, yes. But she could have got him killed,' Peter said. 'Or am I going mad?'

'I don't know what to think,' Jende said. 'This man is supposed to be the murderer. Now he is killed. That means there is another murderer. How many will one case throw up?'

Peter shook his head. Violence was like that. It seemed to set off a chain of events. Himal had killed for revenge. Who would kill Himal?

'But she would not kill her own brother, no?' Jayshree asked.

Jende shrugged. He had often said to Peter that there was no such thing as a criminal type. There were people who gave in to the impulse when the opportunity presented itself and there were those who didn't.

Himali was not asleep but she was in a flowered nightie. When she saw them, it was as if someone had thrown a switch inside her, turning her on to alert mode.

'So late?' she said. 'I am alone, my brother is...'

Then she looked at them again.

'Madam, this is about your brother. And we have a lady police with us.'

Himali backed away from the door. 'Sit down,' she said. 'One minute and I will come.'

They went into the living room, which had been emptied. The furniture was gone. Instead, there were six plastic chairs of the kind common at public meetings. A feeble attempt at style had been made: two were red, two blue and two white.

When she came out again, she was wearing a salwar kameez and her hair was done in two plaits.

'Tell,' she said.

'I am sorry to inform you that your brother was murdered today.'

Himali looked at them wide-eyed and then a shudder ran through her frame.

'Oh God, oh God, I knew he would go like that one day,' she said and buried her face in her dupatta. Jayshree went over and sat down next to her. Were there manuals and procedures for these moments? Was one allowed to hug the bereaved, for instance? Could Jayshree Patil find it in herself to hug a bereaved woman? She solved the problem by going off to the kitchen and filling a steel tumbler with water. She gave it to Himali who took it mechanically and simply held on to it.

'But what could I do? What could I do?' Himali was hiccupping through her sobs. 'Mumma would not correct him. He was her Himmu-Himmu-Himmu. Always him. Only him. Her Kohinoor, she said. And then he became like that. No one could...Not even Puppa...Nothing we said. Nothing we did.'

They waited in silence. After a while, she looked at the water and took a sip. Then she set it down and got up.

'I will wash my face,' she said. When she returned, she was more composed.

'How did he die?'

Jende ignored the question. 'Please identify this photograph,' he said, taking a polaroid out of his pocket.

'That is my brother, Himal Jugalkishore Shah,' said Himali.

'I'm sorry you had to see this, but we have procedures. Your brother was killed a few hours ago. Did he tell you where he was going when he left today?'

Himali looked at him steadily.

'Did you tell your wife where you are going today?' she

turned to Peter. 'Or you? Even you, Madam Inspector, does your husband know?'

Patil shrugged, accepting her promotion gracefully. 'In our line, who can tell where we'll go and what we'll do?'

'Maybe your husband asks once, twice and when you don't answer, then he says, chalo, she does not know herself so she cannot tell.'

Patil looked at Jende and he came to her rescue.

'Is that what you're saying, Mrs Patel? That your brother did not tell you because he did not know?'

Himali considered that.

'No,' she said.

'Then how come you don't know?'

'My brother was not like other people, Inspector. You know that. You saw him. You met him. Everyone who met him, he *phasaoed*. He had them in his spell. They wanted to help him. They wanted to look after him. They would say: come work with me. They would say: come live here and be my paying guest and many of them would not take any money. My brother could have had anything he wanted. But he was not like that.'

Here comes the standard disclaimer about how good and wonderful he was, thought Peter.

'Not like what?' Jende asked.

'He was not able to keep in the good books with anyone. He would make friends like that'—and here she snapped her fingers in the air—'but then there would be a fight. Someone might say something, anything, like "Come on, time" or "Get a hair-cut" and he would start shouting at them. Puppa told him so many times when he was in school: your temper will finish you one day. It was not so bad before, but in the last few years, after he came to Bombay, it became frightening. You had to be careful. He was always ready to explode. I think Puppa's warning came true. It finished him. I think that is why he died.'

'Your brother was murdered,' Jende reminded her. He seemed almost outraged on behalf of the dead man. Perhaps that was what powered him, thought Peter, what made him such a dedicated policeman: that injustice could still affect him deeply.

'I know that. Do you know what it is like, Inspector? First, my mother dies. Then my husband is killed. Then my brother goes.'

'Your husband killed himself, no?' Jayshree asked. 'Sad case.'

'My husband did not kill himself,' said Himali. 'He was killed. He was killed in front of my eyes. Here. By my brother. Now I can tell.'

There was a cold silence in the room. Another murder, Peter thought. Another dead murderer.

Himali drank her glass of water now. She was palpably pleased with the response.

'Maybe you should tell the story from the beginning,' Jayshree said.

'You will understand, sister,' said Himali to Patil. 'Or maybe you will not be able to understand because when you get married you have certain expectations, no? Your husband will do this, your husband will do that. But what if your husband does not put one hand on you?'

Jayshree looked puzzled and then understanding dawned. 'He was a sixer?'

Sixer. Chhakka. Peter could never understand how this cricketing term had come to be used for a hijra. Common wisdom held that it was because the hijras made their rounds on the sixth day of the week. Peter had not noticed this to be particularly true; they seemed to be there all the time. He had never used the expression himself, but all around him men used it to demean other men. And here, now, was a woman doing it.

'Now who can say? He's gone there,' Himali said and pointed to the heavens. 'When the proposal came, we thought our prayers had been answered. The boy was working in Bombay, he had his own place, he had a good job in a foreign bank, he was earning this much, he had a car—all this we were told. And they did not want dowry because the father was a Gandhi-type and the dead mother was also Gandhi-type. I had my suspicions. In this day and age, who does Gandhigiri? But my brother had moved to Bombay then and he said he had seen the boy and I should marry and because her Himmu said so, my mother also said I should marry, and anyway, where did we have the money? Then I met him when he came to his family house in Surat and he was all right. He was handsome and fair and he seemed kind so I said yes and we got married. What dreams I had then, Inspector saahab.'

Bollywood-speak, Peter noticed, although he was riveted by the tale.

'I wanted a child of my own. A good family life. I was willing to give up everything for that. But nothing was happening. On the first day, I thought, he is tired. But on the honeymoon in Nainital, nothing. I thought he was shy. But he was not even trying. He kept giving one excuse or the other. One day it was, I have a boil there. One day it was, the doctor has said I have too much stress, I must take it easy. Another day, pressure of work. I thought, maybe it is true, he comes home so late every night. And he was taking good care of all of us. He was sending money to Mumma, my brother came whenever he liked to eat and sleep here. He liked giving gifts, I could ask for anything, and Himal also. When Mumma was ill, he was very sad, like her own son. We had to bring her to Bombay for dialysis. When you have your mother in your house and your husband does not object, you have to accept some things. So I accepted and I did not say anything.

'That way he was good. He was fond of Mumma because his own had died when he was young. When we were told her kidneys were failing and there was only one thing to do—kidney transplant—it was he who said: Let us do it. And this Himal told my husband: Open an account with me and we will put our money together. He agreed and both of them put their money in the same account. I don't know how much was whose. I had some money, I put that also. The hospital told us we had two, three months.'

'To buy someone's kidney?' Jende asked.

Himali paused as if to think up a lie. Then she decided against it.

'What is there to hide now? There was a poor woman who was saying she would give a kidney. That hospital found her, they did that regularly, everyone knows. But that woman, *kya bataoon*! These people are also too cunning now. They want this and they want that. But we agreed to everything and we kept on putting money away.'

It was easy to piece together the rest. Not long before the operation, Sooraj had fallen into the honey trap. When he was whisked off to the police station, he had cracked completely. He had not locked his phone and had laid himself open to steady blackmail. Peter wasn't sure how much of this Himali knew. How much of it would she reveal? He saw Jende's face was impassive. He would let the woman speak—the truth or lies, he would let it happen.

'Lakhs we had saved for Mumma's kidney and operation,' Himali was saying. 'That day I and my brother took Mumma to the hospital, but there they said, what operation, what theatre, what booking, what bed? There was nothing.

'We came home but Sooraj was not there. He was at work, we thought. We called the bank but he was not there. We were waiting for him when suddenly Mumma's condition went bad. We had to take her back to the hospital, we had to beg, we had to plead and they gave her an ordinary bed in a ward and she died there. From the hospital only Himal took her body to the *shamashan ghat* and did the *kriyakaram* and lit her pyre. I was at home when Sooraj came. I told him, you tell me everything. You did not deposit any money, you did not do any booking. What happened? Tell me the truth, whatever it is. I am not blaming you, I told him, just tell me. It was not a lie. I wanted to know. That was all.

'But then Himal came home and he was very angry. Only two people could withdraw from that account: my husband and he. He had not taken the money. So it had to be Sooraj. He gave him one slap on this side and his head went like that and then he gave him another slap. *Baap re*, I thought, his head will fly off. Sooraj was crying, he fell at Himal's feet, pleading with him, *mujhe maaf kar do, mujhe maaf kar do*. I told Himal, "What is done is done" and he seemed like he was listening to me. My brother has not forgiven anyone even for not giving him food on time. But I tried and he cooled down a bit. He also said, "Now what can we do? The money is gone. Our mother is gone." He told my husband to come into the bedroom and explain everything. I was worried he would beat him again but Sooraj said, "I won't be able to talk in front of you, it is better if I talk to him alone." I came out and sat right here. I could not hear what they were saying. I felt I should know so I went to the kitchen to make tea. I could hear a little from there. My husband was telling Himal about some policemen, Pagmat and one other name...'

'Durra?'

'Maybe. I cannot remember, but I remember Sooraj saying something about some Proxy or something.'

So that was how Himal had tracked down the men who he believed had taken his mother's life. He had shaken the truth out of his brother-in-law.

'I went in with the tea and Sooraj was sitting on the floor

and he was crying again. I felt sorry for him. He was my husband, whatever he may have been. I told Himal to let it go, what could he do now and what could he say? Then my brother, *my own brother*, can you imagine? He grabbed me by the hair and pushed me away. I ran out and stayed in the kitchen. I just prayed for it to end. Maybe I did not pray properly because it did end but in a way that I could never have imagined.

'When they came out, Himal was cool. He said that he wanted an apology from my husband. He told my husband to sit at the table and write a letter to me. He said, "Write: I am sorry. It is my fault. Please forgive me." My husband started writing but Himal grabbed the paper and tore it up. "Write what I told you to write," he said and he slapped my husband, once, twice on the back of the head. I said, "Don't do that, the *chhota magaj* is there, he may die." But he kept slapping and saying, "Write what I tell you and we will forgive you." My husband did not have strength. He was a *lallu*. He wrote. When he had finished, it was as if my brother went mad again. He picked my husband up by his shirt from the back like he was one puppy and threw him against the wall and beat him and beat him and beat him. My husband had even stopped crying, no sound came out of him, like he had lost his voice. His nose and lips were bleeding. Then he tried to get away and he ran into the balcony and my brother picked him up and just like that threw him. Out. Out of the balcony. I began to cry but he said, "If you say anything about this you will go like that too." He told me to go to the bedroom and pretend I was sleeping and when the neighbours come, I must act like I am shocked and so that was what I did.'

There was a moment of total silence.

'Why was he living at Leslie's?'

'He had come to Bombay a year before I got married.

When I came I said he could save money and stay with my husband and me but he said he had found a good PG place close to his work. He said that the man would adopt him, that he treated him like a son.'

This was pushing it, thought Peter. Had Himal really hoped to be Leslie's heir? Or was he merely creating a story for the family? It was difficult to say.

'This is my brother, Inspector saahab. This is my brother I am talking about. I feared his anger. But I did not know he could do something like that. When they took the body, he was sitting with Sooraj's phone and making a note of the numbers. He was calling some numbers and writing down names, I think. I asked him what he was doing and he said, "If you ask too many questions, you know what will happen to you," and he looked toward that balcony. Then two-three days after he killed my husband, someone called and told him to come somewhere. I think he was pretending to be my husband because he was saying, "How will I get so much money?" and "I will come, don't worry. Somehow I will make *bandobast*".'

She was silent for a while. Then she said, 'I think he killed that boy, Inspector saahab. I think so. He killed that boy and he took out his kidney. After I saw how he threw my husband out of the balcony, I can believe he did that.'

Nineteen

Unit called the next morning.

'Uncle, what is happening in this city?' he asked. 'One by one, they are killing people.'

'I know,' Peter said, reminded of his fear for the boy and now surprised by it.

'I think I should go away, this place is becoming dangerous,' Unit said.

Peter thought this might be a good idea.

'Who was that?' Millie asked, bringing him a second cup of tea so he could give her company. He brought her up to date. She shook her head.

'You know, in an Agatha Christie book, she always makes you think that some character has committed the murder and then that character gets killed so he can't have done it and you have to start again.'

'I wish it worked that way,' Peter said. 'There's little doubt that it was Himal who killed Proxy. I think we were right.'

Millie sipped her tea.

'What was he doing in that same toilet again?'

It was a good question. Peter gave up the idea of catching up on sleep and went to the police station, where Zurale was making a list of the numbers that Himal had called.

'So far, her story is working out,' said Jende. 'The number was in use after Sooraj's death. So Himal must have made calls to all these numbers. He registered Sooraj on realcaller.com so he could find out the names behind the numbers.'

'So he did kill. There are two murderers then.'

'Yes. The pathologist says it is not the same knife.'

'How does he know?'

'Something to do with the edges of the wound. Wait one moment. Here,' Jende rustled some papers around and said, 'the edge is like that of a flensing knife.'

'What is that?'

'It is something used to flay animals. Does that help? He is a butcher, this one.'

'Better not say that,' Peter said. Mahim was a wonderful neighbourhood, offering the possibility of prayer at Sheetaladevi, one of the oldest of the city's goddesses, a gurdwara down the road from where the Citylight Cinema had once stood, a dargah and two churches. From the police point of view, though, this was not quite as wonderful.

Jende said, 'One more thing.'

Peter waited.

'According to the forensic people, this time it is not a first-time killer. He has done this before.'

'Good grief.'

'Yes, good grief. But they say it is a hypothesis only. They say this time there was no hesitation. The wound was clean and made in one go.'

Zween, thought Peter. This one went *zween*. And Himal had been killed in the way he had killed. Again, there was something of the Greek tragedy about it. Greek tragedy in a Mumbai public toilet. It didn't get more post-modern.

'What was Himal doing that night in the toilet?'

'Arre, this kind of question you should ask your friend Leslie.'

Suddenly, Peter was tired. Another trip to Bandra.

~

Leslie was all agog.

'Cover his face, mine eyes dazzle. He died young,' he said. 'Poor fellow. He did seem to have that incandescent quality, as if he weren't meant to live long. What a spectacular way to go. Look, he's made the front pages of the papers.'

Peter wanted to point out that Himal had indeed made the front pages, but of the tabloids, then he thought this would be far too much of a fine point for Leslie. Instead, he pushed aside the strange emotions that had suddenly arisen and asked the question that was worrying him: 'What could he be doing in that same toilet?'

Leslie shrugged. 'Strange as it may seem to me, I believe these places are sometimes used to relieve the bladder.'

Peter smiled. From his memory of the world of work, he had sometimes stopped to use a public toilet but only if he were not within reach of a cleaner facility, either at the office or at home. So why would Himal go there, go to a public toilet when he was not working, when he could go at home?

Unless, of course, he was in there for work.

'Do we have a nice picture of him?' Leslie asked.

Peter nodded, and then he remembered Rocket, who had promised information for two thousand.

Leslie threw his hands high in the air when Peter told him.

'Peter, Peter. You trusted that boy? He'll pull snow up his pretty nose and find enough sheikhs to make ten times as much in a night. You may hear from him next Christmas, if you're lucky. Some things are best left to Rani Maa. We'll hit the streets again tonight and ask some questions.'

Peter sighed, but in his heart. When this was over, he was going to take Millie and go to Goa for a long vacation. They would sit in the sun on the porch of his old home in Moira...once they had cleaned it up. No, that would be too much like work. And he sighed again.

~

Leslie was in high spirits that evening.

'I made some inquiries of my own,' he said mysteriously. 'I have not been sitting idle all day as you probably have.'

'In the community?'

'You know, gay men are not completely obsessed with being gay. I went to the Pathfinders Pathology Laboratory and had a blood test. A total waste of time and good blue blood but it was of great help. Himal had lost his job, did you know? He had borrowed money from every assistant in the laboratory even when he had the job. Was the boy addicted to money? I admit I did not dress him in gold, but he got a few thousand now and then. More in the last month or two, when he would ask every second day and walk around in tight chaddis so that I couldn't say no. I'm quite sure he'd lost some other source of good money.'

Peter raised an eyebrow.

'Oh I have no illusions, darling, that there were others who kept him. And in better style, too. My *tijori* is small, though you wouldn't guess from my scarves. The boy had expensive habits, and I think he'd become desperate lately, if he was begging money from laboratory assistants. No surprise if he was visiting railway toilets now. That is what I think. But we shall seek confirmation in the netherworld.'

'Well done,' said Peter. Leslie had uncovered what he and Jende could not.

'Can you imagine? Apparently three people had already come to talk about this one boy.'

'Jende and I went. Who was the third?'

Leslie looked annoyed. 'I didn't think it was important.'

'Probably isn't,' Peter said, though he filed it away for the future.

'Come along, now. We're going to talk to Taxi-Taxi. He's coming to pick us up,' said Leslie.

'Who's that?'

'I don't know why I didn't think of him earlier. He's a walking dictionary on all things gay.'

'He knows more than you?' Peter let his surprise show.

'It is right of you to be shocked,' said Leslie. 'I knew a lot about the scene once. It could have been said I *was* the scene. But I retired a little while ago to my porn stash and my memories.'

'Or when that young clerk broke your heart?'

'Forget I ever told you that story, Peter. Please,' he said and his voice had no trace of the flippant in it. 'I loved. I lost. 'Nuff said.'

Peter had often wished that Leslie would put down his pose and be himself. Now that Leslie had, he wished for the pose in place again. It was easier so.

A black and yellow taxi drew up outside the gate and tooted. Leslie and Peter went out. Leslie got in at the front and was greeted effusively.

'Hello, dear,' said a cheerful voice when Peter got in. The man in the rear-view mirror was balding and had the look of a small-time businessman. His eyes were friendly, however.

'This is Taxi-Taxi,' said Leslie. 'This is my friend Peter.'

'This name I have been given because I own two taxis and I sometimes cruise in one.'

'I have never understood that,' said Leslie to the air.

'Some men like,' said Taxi-Taxi. 'Maybe it's the uniform.'

'There's a uniform?'

'If you own the taxi, you wear white. If you're driving it for someone else, you wear khaki.'

'You don't own this taxi?'

'I do. But my licence has the other number. And khaki gets more gay *giraahaks* than white.'

'Must be because they think of the cops,' said Leslie.

'You do this for a living?' Peter asked.

'Arre no baba, not for living, for enjoying,' said Taxi-

Taxi and Peter laughed as he knew he was expected to and repeated it for good measure: 'Not for living, for enjoying.'

Leslie rolled his eyes.

'I do clothes ka business. Wholesale,' said Taxi-taxi in his self-conscious Hinglish. It was obviously an affectation because he frequently slipped into perfect English.

'We're not about to ask for discounts,' said Leslie.

They were driving slowly around Bandra now.

'Would you be picking up someone now?'

'No,' said Taxi-Taxi. 'Too early. You have to wait until later. That's when there are single men on the road.'

Peter didn't know how this worked. In his world, one hailed taxis.

'There are boys who are going home late, from Cuffe Parade or Colaba, they are walking to Churchgate Station. I stop and I say I am going that way, come sit, and I pat the seat next to me, and they get the idea. Sometimes I have to drop them right home, sometimes only until the station, depends on what they want.'

Peter found that he still had it in him to be shocked.

'In a taxi?'

'Haan, there was a time when I had *kaala* film on the windows. I would roll up the *khidki* and turn on the air-conditioning and play some music. I have very good taste in music. I make my own compilations. *Mughal-e-Azam*. And *Umrao Jaan*. But Muzaffar Ali's film, aahn? Not this new nonsense. And *Mausam hai aashiqana* from Pakeezah. These always set the mood. But now there's one stupp-id rule that you can't have dark film on your windows so it is more difficult, but you can manage if you are creative.'

Peter was still not sure what exactly could happen in a taxi but decided not to inquire. Instead, he handed over the picture of Himal.

'This one?' said Taxi-Taxi. 'We call him *Patthar ke sanam*.

Bad news, very bad news. He's new here. A business friend of mine bought him regularly for his parties in Cuffe Parade, loaned him to others. He was a hit. Sometimes ten thousand a night, more if they tied him up. Then they tired of him. Got aggressive, began asking for too much. Now he takes boys to Paththarwadi...'

'Where is that?' Peter asked.

'It's those stones they put on Marine Drive, na?'

'The tetrapods?'

'Yes, when the tide is down, it's a good place to go. So he phasaaos them in the toilets, on the trains and he takes them to Pattharwadi and he pulls their pants down as if he is hot for them and then he grabs hold of their pants and begins to tear, *thirrr*. That sound is scary, if you think about it. Means you are going to walk home with your bums showing. Who wants that? And now that same body which was so exciting looks frightening. Then he takes their money and watch and anything they have.'

He handed the picture back.

'So sad, no? I always tell the new boys: you have to be very careful if they have muscles. Muscles are like advertising. What you see is not what you get.'

'I didn't know that about Himal,' said Leslie, annoyed. 'See? What happens when you trust somebody?'

'You trusted him with what?'

'I took him as a paying guest. Only he didn't pay much.'

'That is not trust,' said Taxi-Taxi, 'that is lust.'

'You may have a point there.'

'And he speaks English, this one, so he has an advantage.'

Peter must have looked puzzled, for both hastened to explain.

'Cheaters, na? they come from the lower class generally. One should not say it but that is the way it is. Leslie will tell you that I don't have any class consciousness.'

'This is the most democratic taxi in the whole of our fair city,' said Leslie. 'I have seen waiters and cleaning boys in the front seat of this cab.'

'You have to admit they have better bodies than middle-class *bandas*,' said Taxi-Taxi.

'You were saying?' Peter said.

'Most of these boys are from the lower class, the cheaters. So if someone is speaking English, you will assume that he is not a cheater. You will take it that he wants to have sex with you. So what if you're fifty-eight and fat and he's twenty-eight and has a great body? You can pretend to yourself that he wants you. So you do a little more than usual. You take him home instead of to a one-hour hotel. *Finish*. That's it. I even heard of a diamond trader who came to that toilet under the flyover at Marine Drive, remember?'

Leslie nodded.

'Haan, he stopped his car outside and brought the briefcase inside and took one boy with him to Gai-waadi where they have those one-hour rooms. And the boy took the briefcase and went off. Back to wherever he had come from, Burhanpur or Jhumritalaiya or wherever. This is what lust can do.'

'Did that really happen?' Leslie asked.

'Who knows? I've heard this story so often it must be true,' he said and began to hum a tune from *Thodisi Bewafai*.

'How do cheaters get started?' Peter asked.

'See, what happens is that one of these boys is working at some *balta* job in the city. Say, he's a cleaner, or a peon or something. And one of the older ones will tell him there is money to be made if he doesn't mind coming out in the night. Most times, they will not talk directly about what they call homosex. They will say it has to do with fooling someone, phasaaoing and making some rich old man an *ullu*. That will get them started and when someone makes a pass, both the boys will jump on him and get some money. There are many different ways. Some boys will go home with a client and even let him play with them a bit or whatever and then they will say, "I am not putting on my clothes again unless you pay" or "I will scream and call your neighbours unless you pay" or something like that. It's blackmail, but it's a one-time thing. There are lots of people out there who will pay. And some even pay and say to the boy, "Come again, next week." This boy, what is his name?'

'Himal.'

'Himal? Okay, whatever. I heard different. Anyway, he must have also come to the city and must have seen how much money there is here. You read in the papers, na? Someone paid this much for a painting. Someone was caught with jewellery worth that much at the airport. For you and for me, these are just numbers. For boys like him, they are like whips. They want that money. And in most cases, the only thing they have is the body. So they will put the body on the market because they have seen all those Hindi movies where the *shaukeen* are willing to pay so much for fresh *maal*. Then they find that this is also just a story; the body is also cheap. It doesn't have that much value. Nothing has much value. Men who pay like that, pay that much, they don't fall in love. They want a new body every day, if possible. This is how the poor boys go bad.'

'How long has he been at this?'

'At Pattharwadi? Not long. *Naya banda hai*. Not much time, I am told, since he came down in life and got here, but already he is famous. I keep telling Vikram, put one gallery on gaybombay.com and say these are the people who are doing bad things like that. I will take the pictures, I've told him. But that lawyer friend of his says they might sue. Just imagine. The cheek! *Ulta chor kotwal ko daante*. If you have another copy of this guy's picture, I will keep it with my gallery of rogues.'

He opened the glove compartment and took out a phone and handed it over to Leslie who began to flick his finger across the screen, making dismissive comments as he went. 'Oh look at that one! Who does she think she is? Who would go for that little number?'

He handed the phone over to Peter as they drove South over Lady Jamshedji's causeway to Mahim. Peter flipped through the pictures and stopped when he saw Unit.

'This one? You know this one?'

'Oh that's a dangerous one, all right,' shuddered Taxi-taxi. 'I call him Mack the Knife. He brings a knife along with him and he cuts straight through your shirt and then cuts your skin lightly, gently, so you begin to bleed. For most queens, this is enough to terrify them. He works that dark stretch underneath Mahatma Gandhi Swimming Pool.'

'Unit?'

'Haan, he's very good with a knife. You know how he got his name, na?'

'No.'

'He worked with the Dissection Unit of the Veterinary Laboratory at Parel. His job was to flay the carcasses of the dead animals.'

Twenty

Jende listened to all that Peter had to say without any expression. He did not seem convinced but Peter sometimes felt it would take a smoking gun to persuade his friend. However, at the end of it, he did send Zurale to bring Unit in for questioning.

Jende began easily.

'Tell me about yourself, after you finished school, what did you do?'

'I went to Parel College for BA.'

'Did you finish it?'

'No, sir, I had family problems.'

'And then what did you do?'

'I did a course in physical training.'

'And did you work as a physical trainer?'

'No, sir. There are no jobs.'

'Where else did you work?'

'Here and there.'

'Hmmm. Any particulars?'

'Nothing for very long. All small-small jobs only.'

'Were you ever employed at the Veterinary College in Parel?'

Unit looked startled.

'No, sir. I mean, yes, sir.'

'What was your job there?'

'I was laboratory assistant.'

'What did you do?'

'Whatever I was told.'

'Were you ever in charge of flaying carcasses?'

'Yes, sir.'

'What did that entail?'

'When an animal dies because of disease or something and it is sent to us, someone has to cut off its skin and inject it with formaldehyde so it does not begin to rot. Then it is put in cold storage till a veterinary doctor can do an examination.'

'You were good at this job?'

'There is nothing to be good or bad at, sir. It is a job.'

'How long did you do it?'

'Two years.'

'After that?'

'I got tired, sir. And I left.'

'How did you make a living after that?'

Unit looked at Peter, then decided to lie. 'I am a personal trainer now.'

'Where were you last night?'

'I was at home, sir. I had a bad headache.'

'Anyone with you?'

'Yes, sir, three other boys. We live together. I was with my family but I moved out, it got too crowded.'

'These boys, they also do this personal training?'

'No, sir. One is a peon and two are couriers.'

'Give me their numbers,' said Jende. Unit flicked through his phone and read off three names and three numbers. Jende noted them down carefully and handed them over to Zurale.

'Do you know this person?'

He pushed a photograph of Himal over the table.

'No, sir.'

'He was also killed last night,' said Jende.

'Arre-re-re,' said Unit. 'What a city this is becoming.'

'Will you get his kidney too?'

'Sir, what you're saying, sir? His kidney was not taken out.'

'And who told you that?'

Unit hesitated.

'It was in the papers.'

'Was it? In which paper?'

'Maybe on television.'

'Maybe. Which channel?'

'I don't know. I see so many. Marathi channels, you know. So many there are.'

'There are many, yes. We can check all of them. All we have to do is get what the news anchors are reading. You know they read it from a screen, no? So we will get everything the news anchors are reading and see where they say: Himal Shah's kidney was not taken.'

'Sir, I think they did not say it like that. But if his kidney had been taken, they would have said that. They always give that kind of news.'

'That is not what you said earlier. You said you heard it on the news that his kidney was not taken. Who said this? And where?'

'Sir, why you're doing like this?'

'I am not doing anything. Not yet, anyway. Do you carry a knife?'

'No, sir.'

'Do you have a knife at home?'

'No sir.'

'Not even to cook?'

'Like that of course we have a knife.'

'We are going to search your house, you know that.'

'Sir, I live with three-three boys. They may have knives and then you will blame me?'

'We are also going to ask them whether they can be sure you were at home all night.'

'Sir, I can only hope they will tell the truth. Please can I have some water?'

'Do you think one of them will lie?'

'Sir, who can tell?'

'Or will they all lie for you?'

'No, sir, they are from good families. Please, sir, some water.'

'Would you lie for them?'

'No, sir. I am also from a good family.'

Jende nodded. 'This I can see.'

Peter went to get a glass of water.

'Who is it for?' Zurale asked.

'For me,' Peter lied because he could not be sure they would give him the water otherwise.

Zurale picked up a bottle of mineral water and poured him a glass tumbler full. Peter took it back. Jende frowned but said nothing when he set it in front of Unit.

'Did you know this Himal Shah?'

'No, sir.'

'You're sure?'

'Yes, sir.'

'Do you know this man?'

He pushed across a picture of Proxy.

'Sir, I have already told you. His name is Proxy. He was my friend.'

'He died the kind of death he deserved.'

'No, sir. Why you're saying things like that sir?'

'Because it is the truth. Do you know what his job was?'

Unit was silent.

'He had sex with men.'

Unit stayed silent but it was an effort.

'He was a common randi.'

'No, sir. It was not like that. You know it well.'

'Do I?'

'Yes. Your men, policemen. They spoiled him. They told him, go and show yourself and then when they try to touch you, we will catch them. Your men made him like that. If they had not made him do these things, he would not be dead.'

'He could have refused,' said Jende but his voice was quiet now, almost gentle. In comparison, Unit's got harsher, stronger.

'Oh? So easy? The police tell you to do something, you do it. You know that. I know that. Proxy also knew it. And he told me when that man came with the briefcase, he told them, my mother-in-law is ill, don't take all the money. He begged them. But they said, *saale chhakke*, if your mother-in-law is ill why are you coming to do kela massage in a toilet? They gave him his phone and said, we saw, we have all your numbers, your office number, your home number, now we know where you work, we know where you live. And they kept calling him, telling him to come with more and more money. They took all his money and he killed himself.'

'He did not kill himself. This Himal killed him,' Jende said.

'He killed his own brother-in-law? He made his own sister vidhva? Then I am glad I...'

'You are glad you what?'

But Unit froze and said nothing. Then with a movement so sudden that no one could have expected it, he smashed his head on to the glass tumbler, crushing it and scratching his head on the splinters so that blood flowed down his face. He began to scream and scream.

Zurale burst into the room.

'Sir, he said it was for him,' he said looking at Peter accusingly.

'Don't worry, he's my friend. He thought we would not even give this fellow water,' said Jende. 'But he got a lesson in police brutality.'

'Sorry, sorry, sorry,' said Peter.

Peter thought he would be in the doghouse but Jende seemed to take the whole morning in his stride.

'You go home now,' he said. 'In the evening, we will go and see these friends of his and see if he really has an alibi.'

'I can give evidence that you didn't...'

Jende relented. 'We have CCTV in the interrogation room. It will be recorded what he did and what I didn't do. But next time, tell Zurale who it is for and he will give you a plastic glass.'

Peter felt a wave of relief wash over him. Then it struck him.

'CCTV!' he said.

'Haan?'

'There's CCTV on Matunga Road. They might have caught Unit coming into the station, even on his way to the toilet.'

'Or out of it,' Jende said.

Zurale cast his eyes up to the stars. He could see another painful detail coming up.

Peter seized the opportunity.

'Can I talk to him?'

'If you want,' Jende said. 'But anything he says to you will be of no use to us. So don't ask him to confess.'

Peter went back into the room where a constable was bandaging up Unit. A laboratory attendant was carefully cleaning Unit's nails. Peter did not look too carefully but he saw what she was looking for and had found: rusty stains of blood beneath his fingernails. Himal's blood. Unit had not washed as much as he should have. Perhaps he should have gone to Pagmat's bathroom and learned how to clean himself.

'Chacha!'

His tone was very different now. He was confident, almost cocky.

'Why did you do that?'

'Why not?' Unit laughed. 'They're *pandus*, all of them. They think they're too great. *Vardi dala* and they think they're Amitabh Bachchan.'

He was slumped in his chair, his legs splayed, his body language totally assured.

'I was talking to Rocket about you.'

'Rocket? *Choot hai sala*,' he said. Then he stopped and looked at Peter. 'What did he say?'

'Good things. He told me about that time you beat up that Chinese guy.'

Unit tilted his head.

'*Chinese-binese kuchh nahin tha*. He was from Sikkim. Kya, Uncle, what will happen to our country if you educated people are saying our *desh ka banda* is Chinese?'

Peter nodded to acknowledge the hit.

'But Proxy just ran away, didn't he?'

'Who told you that?' Unit's face went serious.

'Who else? Rocket.'

'It wasn't like that. Proxy was a good guy. He was not going to run.'

'Rocket says he ran and left you to get the pasting.'

'Rocket knows nothing.'

'Then what happened that evening?'

'Nothing happened. Some *haathapaai*. He hit, I hit. That's all. And Proxy did not run away.'

'You were good friends, you and Proxy.'

'Like,' Unit said and his voice trembled. He was quiet. Peter waited.

'Like that,' Unit spoke again, putting up two fingers, twined around each other.

'He should not have died like that.'

'No,' said Unit. 'No one should die like that. Not in a toilet.'

Peter thought of the young man who had made that very toilet the scene of his work life.

'I know, Uncle. He was doing bad things.'

The image of Unit with kaajal in his eyes, his T-shirt tight, his jeans...

'I know what you're thinking: I also do this dhanda.'

Peter tried to say something in his own defence.

'It's okay, Uncle. When I become a father, I would not like my son to do what I do. But my business is simple. I do bad things, you could say. But the police? When the police take your phone and say bring thousand rupees or you'll go to the court tomorrow and everyone will know who you are—that is a crime. I told Proxy: don't do that. I earn well sometimes, we will save and do some other business. But he didn't listen. Those men gave him the taste for fast money and he would say: I have the police to protect me.'

Unit laughed but it was not a pleasant sound.

'See how much they protected him.'

Peter nodded. He tried to bring himself to ask the question that was uppermost in his mind.

'I know what you want to know, Uncle.'

'What is it I want to know?'

'You want to know whether something you said showed me who had killed Proxy.'

Peter was startled at the young man's perspicacity. It was what he had been wondering, whether he had been careless in some conversation he'd had with Unit, whether he had let something slip and somehow brought Himal to his death. He did not think he had, he did not remember anything, and yet there was the worm of doubt...

'No, it was not anything you said. You gave Rocket his photo, you remember? You told him where he worked. Rocket gave the job to me for a commission. I saw the photo and I recognized him. Who will forget that kind of face and body? I had seen him in the toilet sometimes. I went to the lab as his friend and I found out he gave injections. Then I knew. He had killed the boy. He had killed Proxy.'

So Unit was the other person who had visited the laboratory. Suddenly Peter felt very tired. He sank back into his chair.

'I understand why this Himal was doing what he was doing. I would do like that too. He wanted *badla*. He wanted to finish everyone. He didn't know that Proxy wanted to give him back the money. How could he? You know, Uncle, Proxy was telling me that he was worried about that fellow's suicide. He said: Unit, *tu jaa*. Find out, na. Go. No one will trust me. I said, No one will trust me either. Then I got an idea: we will send Sunil-bhaiyya; and so we called your son, but his phone was switched off. But even before that could happen, this fellow had killed Proxy. It was my fault. He said: Unit, come with me, let us go and give back this much money at least. But I said: What is the point? The old lady is dead. Forget it, don't get involved any more. I stopped him, Uncle. That is why he was killed.'

'You should not feel that way. Himal killed him...'

'Uncle, the world can think like that. My mother can say: it was his karma, what can you do? I don't know all this philosophy. I know one thing. He was my yaar. For my yaar, I did what I had to do.'

And Peter felt the weight of what the boy felt; it was not just the affection of a long friendship; maybe it was something close to devotion. Would Unit ever recover from this?

Peter stood up and went to the other side of the table and put a hand on his shoulder. 'It wasn't your job to keep him alive,' he said.

Unit looked up at him as if surprised by his lack of comprehension. He tried to say something, as if to explain and then gave up.

There was silence.

Peter asked: 'So you followed Himal for many days?'

'No, Uncle,' said Unit but with a trace now of cunning. 'One day, I saw him at the toilet and I thought: Now you go the same way.'

'You had the knife with you?'

'I always carry a knife.'

He stood up and looked straight into Peter's eyes.'This is not a confession, Uncle.'

Peter nodded

'I'm sorry, Uncle. You gave me food. You called me home. You treated me good. Your son is also good. I'm sorry that I brought all this to your door.'

Peter looked at Unit, slight of build, his head barely the level of Peter's shoulder, the look in his eyes both defiant and helpless. He thought of the artless way in which the boy had wolfed his food, of his belief that he would get married one day, of the ease with which he had let Peter into his life. He swallowed hard.

'See, Uncle, see what this 377 has done? This world, Uncle. It made Proxy into a criminal. Everybody a criminal, except those *pandus*. So many died, Uncle—laash after laash. Maybe I will also die. Why did anyone have to die, Uncle? Why did my Proxy—'

And he crumpled, his head on Peter's chest, and wept. They wept together then, man and man, and were not ashamed.

Twenty-one

After Jende dropped him home, Peter went to sit on the veranda. Sunil joined him there and looked at his father for a moment, wordlessly. Then he went and brought out the bottle of RC and two glasses.

'A small one,' said Peter.

'Mom?' Sunil called. 'You want one?'

'No. I'll have a Frooti,' she said and came out, with the mango drink decanted into a champagne flute.

Sunil shoved up and Millie settled down. Night began to slip into the city.

Sunil said suddenly, 'I suppose I've been childish. I owe you something. An explanation, perhaps.'

'You owe us nothing,' said Millie evenly. 'But if you want to tell us anything, we're here.'

Peter was suddenly grateful for his wife. He would have tried to work out what the right thing to say would be and might have ended up in an ideological argument with Sunil.

'I fell in love. Okay, I didn't even know I was in love...' Sunil stopped.

Peter hoped it wasn't something in his face. He feared it was, though. What kind of face was one supposed to make?

'Are you sure you want to hear this?'

'If you're sure you want to tell it,' said Peter, uncomfortably aware that he was only echoing Millie's sentiments.

Of course, it was the wrong thing to say. Sunil looked at him almost hostilely.

'I don't want to tell you anything.'

Mille clucked a little. Sunil sighed. 'I know that's wrong. I know you've tried to keep communication channels open. But this is private and probably outside your experience. It isn't easy. I don't know how to talk about it.'

Peter decided that he had better say nothing for the rest of the conversation.

Sunil said, 'Do you remember Roosh?'

'Your best friend in the first standard?' Millie asked. How did she remember all this, Peter wondered. Did it have something to do with being a mother? He could not remember much about his son's life, other than the bare bones of it.

'Yes. He was. I met him again in junior college. And I fell in love with him,' said Sunil.

Peter sat very still and tried not to look at Millie's face. He was relieved that what he felt was only a great sense of relief. He was reminded of a Sunday afternoon seven years ago: Sunil returned from a football match and locked himself in his small room. They let him be at first, and then an hour passed, then another, and when they asked he said from the other side of the door, in a calm, distant voice, that he needed to be alone. Millie and he tried to go about their evening—the morning paper read at night, the shirt ironed for the morning, the rice put to boil. But a huge shadow had covered their world. Then the door opened, Sunil came out and asked for the sports section of the paper and for dinner and a breeze blew and it was light.

'I don't think I would have been able to tell him,' Sunil was saying now. 'But he knew and he said it for both of us. Only…'

He paused, as if collecting his thoughts.

'By then Roosh wanted to become a woman.'

Sunil looked into his glass and was silent, and now Peter

turned to look at Millie. Her face seemed to show nothing but her concern.

'I didn't know what to think. I thought I was going to spend the rest of my life with a man, and at the time I wanted nothing more. I knew I would be happy. Now that man said he wanted to be a woman...I didn't know what to feel. I suppose I was confused. But I wanted to be supportive or something. Only, Roosh's father was really angry and threw him out of the house.'

'You should have brought him here,' Millie said, simply, matter-of-factly, and Peter wondered how they would have responded to this then. Easy to say now. He played the scene out: the knock on the door, the young man with Peter, the explanations...or would there have been explanations? Perhaps they might have stopped somewhere along the way, at an Irani, and invented a story: a missed train, a stolen wallet, he's only staying for a few days...

'He had a better option. He went to New York. His mother was there and she was fine with all this. I think his mother was American. So he had the change there. And he came back as a woman. But only to tell me that he had met someone else. A Puerto Rican, I think it was. That's how it ended,' he said.

'Oh dear.'

Sunil raised his eyebrows and looked at Peter, who went quiet.

'You must have been so hurt,' Millie said.

'I think I was relieved. Roosh had started taking some underground hormones even before he left and he'd become really difficult to deal with. And the twelfth standard was coming up and I had to study for the TISS entrance as well and he was getting cranky all the time.'

He paused and then said: 'But I spent some part of my love life in love with a man who was a woman.'

'Maybe you loved the woman in the man,' said Peter and then immediately regretted it. He felt he sounded like he was trying too hard.

'I kept wondering about that. What did it make me? That's where TISS helped hugely. Because we had a class about gender and sexuality and there was a really nice instructor who told us not to put things in boxes and give names to them. "That's what society does," he said. "You don't have to do it to yourself."'

Peter mentally blessed the teacher.

'I wish you could have told us, Baba,' said Millie.

'I wish I could have told you too,' Sunil said. 'Now that I think of it. But I couldn't. I didn't have the guts.'

'It's not a question of guts. We should have made it possible for you to tell us.'

'Let's not make this a blamefest, Maa,' said Sunil and Peter recorded the word without wanting to. 'I only hope that if I ever have a child, he'll have the guts to tell me and I'll have the ears to listen.'

'Where's Roosh now?' Millie asked.

'Not Roosh. Rinelle. We're friends on Facebook now.'

'Is she with her Puerto Rican?'

'I haven't asked.'

'You could have checked,' said Millie.

Sunil laughed.

'I have the feeling you will,' he said.

'What nonsense,' said Millie crossly.

~

Later that night, Peter said: 'Thank you.'

Millie looked at him as she rubbed cold cream over her face. 'You weren't much help,' she said. Peter took this on the chin. He hadn't been.

'What you said about how he didn't have to tell us anything, but we were here to listen? That was perfect.'

'Enough,' Millie said and picked up her hairbrush.

'It was,' he said. 'I wouldn't have managed that.'

'I kept thinking about it all these days. I didn't want to. I wanted to accept him as he is. But it was very hard. So I rehearsed it.'

He looked at her, respectfully.

'Like an interview,' she continued. 'What if he says this, what am I going to say? What if he says that? I hadn't rehearsed for what he finally told us, though. I hadn't imagined.'

'But it worked.'

The brush stopped mid-air and she turned to look at him.'To be honest, I still don't know what to think.'

Peter sighed. 'Maybe it's like that teacher said. We shouldn't put people in boxes.'

'It's easy to *say*.'

'That's why I don't want a grandchild,' he said. 'All this trying to understand them and accept them and protect them and make decisions for them; it's so much work.'

'Don't talk rubbish,' said Millie shortly. 'It's always so much more than work.'

He thought about it.

'Yes, always,' he said.

She looked at him suspiciously and then decided to believe him.